An A to Z of Modern
Latin American
Literature in English
Translation

An A to Z of Modern Latin American Literature in English Translation

Jason Wilson

First published 1989 by
The Institute of Latin American Studies
31 Tavistock Square, London WC1H 9HA

© The Institute of Latin American Studies

British Library Cataloguing in Publication Data

Wilson, Jason, *1944–*
An A to Z of modern Latin American literature in English
translation.
1. Latin American literatures. Translations into English
language. Bibliographies
I. Title
016.86

ISBN 0–901145–67–X

Typeset by TJB Photosetting Ltd, Grantham, Lincolnshire
Printed by W G Harrison Ltd, Grantham, Lincolnshire

CONTENTS

"Say what one will of its inadequacy, translation remains one of the most important, worthwhile concerns in the totality of world affairs."

Goethe to Carlyle

INTRODUCTION

This checklist is the fruit of years of jotting down details about Latin American literature in English translation on scraps of paper. Apart from reviewing some of the books included I have tried to verify as many of the details as possible in various libraries, especially at University College London, the Canning House library, the University of London Library (Senate House) and the library of the Institute of Latin American Studies, University of London. Earlier lists are gratefully acknowledged in the bibliography at the end. I would like to thank Norman Thomas di Giovanni, Margaret Sayers Peden, Stephen Watts, Helen Lane, Maureen Ahern, Noel Treacy, Tony Bell, Alan Biggins and many others for their help, though, of course, any mistakes or omissions are entirely my responsibility. My rough cut-off date has been 1st July 1989.

I decided on the convenient alphabetical format for the Latin American authors translated. Each entry begins with the author's name, country of birth and dates. This is followed by the English title, genre, translator, publisher, place and date for each translation, ending with the original title and date. In the case of an author with more than one work translated I have listed the works in the date order of the translations. In the few cases where I have not been able to find all the details I have nevertheless included a partial entry, and would appreciate any reader sending me further information. At the end I have added a chronological list (in order of publication) of anthologies of Latin American literature in English translation. By literature I have meant fiction, theatre, and poetry but not interviews or overtly scholarly works. However, if a writer has written essays or memoirs these are included. By Latin American I have meant the Spanish and Portuguese speaking New World since its independence from Europe. Only an entry on Sor Juana breaks my rule. This checklist does not include details such as whether a book is hardback or paperback, the page numbers, or if it is in print or not.

An early intention was to annotate as many entries as possible with excerpts from critics about the failures and successes of the translations. These critical comments diverged along predictable lines, from praise because a translation read well in English, to criticism that another translation betrayed the original or cut out bits, to surprise that a translation read like a translation, 'as if it had remained in the foreign language'. I wanted to focus on the actual translations and translators, rather than what the novels, plays or poems might be about, because I had perceived an injustice in the way translators have been relegated and often even dropped from the credits. To refer to my Goethe epigraph, itself a translation: few of us would have read Dostoevsky, Kafka, Calvino or Kundera without translators. In the future I intend to expand the simple listing in this *A to Z* and examine the quality of the translations and what they reveal about the interplay between English speaking cultures and the Latin American cultures translated.

The actual amount of Latin American literature available today is the tip of an iceberg. In a note in the *Times Literary Supplement* (14–20 July 1989) I touched on this and on some of the trends that emerged while collating my entries, naming some of those writers not yet translated. Finally, I would like to see the teaching of Latin American literature in translation become part of all literary courses in higher education, and I hope that the *A to Z* will help to promote this aim.

Jason Wilson
Department of Spanish, University College, London

A

AGOSÍN, Marjorie (Chile/U.S.A. 1955–)

Brujas y algo más/Witches and Other Things – Poetry. Trans. Cola Franzen. Prol. Elena Poniatowska. Latin American Literary Review Press: Pittsburgh, 1986.

Pablo Neruda – Essay. Trans. Lorraine E. Roses. Twayne Publishers: Boston, 1986.

Women of Smoke – Poetry. Trans. Naomi Lindstrom. Latin American Literary Review Press: Pittsburgh, 1988. *Mujeres de humo*, 1987.

Zones of Pain – Poetry. Trans. Cola Franzen. White Pine Press: New York, 1988.

Women of Smoke – Poetry. Trans. Janice Molloy. Williams-Wallace: Stratford, Ontario, 1989. *Mujeres de humo*, 1987.

AGUIAR FILHO, Adonias (Brazil 1925–)

Memories of Lazarus – Fiction. Trans. Fred P. Ellison. Univ. of Texas Press: Austin, 1969. *Memórias de Lazaro*, 1952.

AGUILAR MALTA, Demetrio (Ecuador 1909–1981)

Manuela, la caballeresa del sol – Fiction. Trans. Willis Knapp Jones. Southern Illinois Univ. Press: Carbondale, 1967. *La caballeresa del sol*, 1964.

Seven Serpents and Seven Moons – Fiction. Trans. Gregory Rabassa. Univ. of Texas Press: Austin, 1979. *Siete lunas y siete serpientes*, 1970.

Don Goyo – Fiction. Trans. John and Carolyn Brushwood. Humana Press: Clifton, NJ, 1980. *Don Goyo*, 1930.

Babelandia – Fiction. Trans. Peter Earle. Humana Press: Clifton, NJ, 1985. *Babelandia*, 1980.

ALBÁN, Laureano (Costa Rica 1942–)

Autumn's Legacy – Poetry. Bilingual. Trans. Frederick H. Fornoff. Ohio Univ. Press: Athens, Ohio, 1982. *Herencia del otoño*, 1980.

The Endless Voyage – Poetry. Trans. Frederick H. Fornoff. Ohio Univ. Press: Athens, Ohio, 1984. *El viaje interminable*, 1981.

ALEGRÍA, Ciro (Peru 1909–67)

Broad and Alien is the World – Fiction. Trans. Harriet de Onís. Farrar & Rinehart: New York, 1941; Nicholson & Watson: London, 1942; Holt, Rinehart & Winston: New York, 1963; Merlin: London, 1983. *El mundo es ancho y ajeno*, 1941.

The Golden Serpent – Fiction. Trans. Harriet de Onís. Signet: New York, 1943. *La serpiente de oro*, 1935.

ALEGRÍA, Claribel (Nicaragua/El Salvador 1924–)

Flowers from the Volcano – Poetry. Bilingual. Trans. Carolyn Forché. Univ. of Pittsburgh Press: Pittsburgh, 1982.

They Won't Take Me Alive. Salvadorean Women in Struggle for National Liberation – Essay. Trans. Amanda Hopkinson. The Women's Press: London, 1986.

Luisa in Realityland – Fiction. Trans. Darwin J. Flakoll. Curbstone Press: Willimantic, Conn., 1987. *Luisa en el país de la realidad*, date unknown.

Woman of the River – Poetry. Bilingual. Trans. Darwin J. Flakoll. Univ. of Pittsburgh Press: Pittsburgh, 1989.

Ashes of Izalco, with Darwin J. Flakoll – Fiction. Curbstone Press: Willimantic, Conn., 1989.

ALEGRÍA, Fernando (Chile 1918–)

Lautaro – Fiction. Trans. Delia Goetz. Farrar & Rinehart: New York, 1944. *Lautaro, joven libertador de Arauco*, 1943.

My Horse González – Fiction. Trans. Carlos Lozano. Las Américas: New York, 1964. *Caballo de copas*, 1958.

The Chilean Spring – Fiction. Trans. Stephen Fredman. Latin American Literary Review Press: Pittsburgh, 1980. *El paso de los gansos*, 1975.

Changing Centuries:Selected Poems – Poetry. Bilingual. Trans. Stephen Kessler. Latin American Literary Review Press: Pittsburgh, 1984.

Instructions for Undressing the Human Race – Poetry. Trans. Matthew Zion and Lennart Bruce. Kayak Books: Santa Cruz, Calif., 1984. *Instrucciones para desnudar a la raza humana*, 1981.

The Funhouse. Trans. Stephen Kessler. Arte Público: Houston, Tex., 1984.

ALENCAR, José Martiniano de (Brazil 1829–77)

Iracema, the Honey-Lips, a Legend of Brazil – Fiction. Trans. Sir Richard and Isabel Burton. Bickers & Son: London, 1886; H. Fertig: New York, 1976. *Iracema*, 1865.

Ubirajara. A Legend of the Tupy Indians. Trans. J.T.W. Sadler. No further details in book.

ALLENDE, Isabel (Chile 1942–)

The House of the Spirits – Fiction. Trans. Magda Bogin. Knopf: New York, 1985; Cape: London, 1985; Black Swan: London, 1986. *La casa de los espíritus*, 1982.

Of Love and Shadows – Fiction. Trans. Margaret Sayers Peden. Knopf: New York, 1987; Cape: London, 1987; Black Swan: London, 1988. *De amor y de sombra*, 1984.

Eva Luna – Fiction. Trans. Margaret Sayers Peden. Knopf: New York, 1988; Hamish Hamilton: London, 1989. *Eva Luna*, 1987.

ALMEIDA, José Américo de (Brazil 1887–1980)

Trash – Fiction. Trans. Robert Scott-Buccleuch. Peter Owen: London, 1978. *A bagaceira*, 1928.

ALMEIDA, Manuel Antônio de (Brazil 1831–61)

Memoirs of a Militia Sergeant – Fiction. Trans. Linton J. Barrett. Pan American Union: Washington, DC, 1959. *Memórias de um sargento de milícias*, 1854.

ALONSO, Luis Ricardo (Spain/Cuba 1929–)

Territorio Libre – Fiction. Trans. Alan Brown. Peter Owen: London, 1967. *Territorio libre*, 1966.

The Candidate – Fiction. Trans. Tania de Gámez. Pocket Books: New York, 1972. *El candidato*, 1970.

ALTAMIRANO, Ignacio (Mexico 1834–93)

El Zarco, the Bandit – Fiction. Trans. Mary Allt. Duchness: New York, 1957; Folio Society: London, 1957. *El zarco*, 1901.

Christmas in the Mountain – Fiction. Trans. & ed. Harvey Johnson. University of Florida Press: Gainesville, 1961. *Navidad en las montañas*, 1871.

AMADO, Jorge (Brazil 1912–)

The Violent Land – Fiction. Trans. Samuel Putnam. Knopf: New York, 1945; Collins Harvill: London, 1989. *Terras do sem fim*, 1942.

Gabriela, Clove and Cinnamon – Fiction. Trans. James L. Taylor and William L. Grossman. Knopf: New York, 1962; Chatto & Windus: London, 1963; Souvenir: London, 1983. *Gabriela, cravo e canela*, 1958.

Home is the Sailor – Fiction. Trans. Harriet de Onís. Knopf: New York, 1964; Chatto & Windus: London, 1964. Avon Books: New York, 1979. *Os velhos marinheiros*, 1961.

The Two Deaths of Quincas Wateryell – Fiction. Trans. Barbara Shelby. Avon Books: New York, 1965. *A morte e a morte de Quincas Berro D'Agua*, 1962.

Shepherds of the Night – Fiction. Trans. Harriet de Onís. Knopf: New York, 1967; Collins Harvill: London, 1989. *Os pastores da noite*, 1964.

Dona Flor and her Two Husbands, a Moral and Amorous Tale – Fiction. Trans. Harriet de Onís. Knopf: New York, 1969; Weidenfeld & Nicolson: London, 1969; Serpent's Tail: London, 1987. *Dona Flor e seus dois maridos*, 1966.

Tent of Miracles – Fiction. Trans. Barbara Shelby. Knopf: New York, 1971; Collins Harvill: London, 1989. *A tenda dos milagres*, 1969.

Tereza Batista: Home from the Wars – Fiction. Trans. Barbara Shelby. Knopf: New York, 1975; Souvenir Press: London, 1982. *Tereza Batista, cansada de guerra*, 1972.

Tieta – Fiction. Trans. Barbara Shelby. Knopf: New York, 1979; Souvenir Press: London, 1981. From *Tiêta do Agreste*, 1977.

Jubiabá – Fiction. Trans. Margaret A. Neves. Avon Books: New York, 1984. *Jubiabá*, 1935.

Sea of Death – Fiction. Trans. Gregory Rabassa. Avon Books: New York, 1984. *Mar morto*, 1936.

Pen, Sword, Camisole: A Fable to Kindle Hope – Fiction. Trans. Helen Lane. Godine: New York, 1985; Avon Books: New York, 1986. *Farda, fardão, camisola de dormir*, 1979.

Showdown – Fiction. Trans. Gregory Rabassa. Bantam: New York, 1988. *Tocaia Grande*, 1984.

Captains of the Sand – Fiction. Trans. Gregory Rabassa. Avon: New York, 1988. *Capitães de areia*, 1937.

AMORIM, Enrique (Uruguay 1900–60)

The Horse and his Shadow – Fiction. Trans. Richard O'Connell and James Graham Luján. Scribner's: New York, 1943. *El caballo y su sombra*, 1941.

ANDERSON IMBERT, Enrique (Argentina 1910–)

Spanish-American Literature: a History – Essay. Trans. John V. Falconieri. Wayne State Univ. Press: Detroit, 1963. *Historia de la literatura hispanoamericana*, 1954.

The Other Side of the Mirror (El grimorio). Short Stories by Enrique Anderson Imbert – Fiction. Trans. Isabel Reade. Southern Illinois Univ. Press: Carbondale, 1966; Macdonald: London, 1968. *El grimorio*, 1961.

ANDRADE, Mário de (Brazil 1893–1945)

Fräulein – Fiction. Trans. Margaret Richardson Hollingworth. MacCauly: New York, 1933. *Amar, verbo intransitivo*, 1927.

Hallucinated City – Poetry. Bilingual. Trans. Jack E. Tomlins. Vanderbilt Univ. Press: Kingston, Tenn., 1969. *Paulicéia desvairada*, 1922.

Macunaíma – Fiction. Trans. E. A. Goodland. Random House: New York, 1984; Quartet: London, 1984. *Macunaíma o herói sem nenhum carácter (Rapsodia)*, 1928.

ANDRADE, Oswald de (Brazil 1890–1954)

Seraphim Grosse Pointe – Fiction. Trans. Kenneth D. Jackson and Albert Bork. Nefertiti Head Press: Austin, Tex., 1979. *Serafim Ponte Grande*, 1933.

The Dead Woman – Fiction. 1980 (other publication details unknown). *A morta*, 1937.

The Sentimental Memoirs of John Seaborne – Fiction. Nefertiti Head Press: Austin, Tex., 1979. *Memórias sentimentais de João Miramar*, 1923.

ANGELO, Ivan (Brazil 1936–)

A Celebration – Fiction. Avon Books: New York, 1982. *A festa*, 1976.

The Tower of Glass – Fiction. Trans. Ellen Watson. Avon Books: New York, 1986. *Casa de vidro: cinco histórias do Brasil*, 1979.

ANJOS, Cyro dos (Brazil 1906–69).

Diary of a Civil Servant – Fiction. Trans. Arthur Brakel. Fairleigh Dickinson Univ. Press: Toronto, 1986. *O amanuense Belmiro*, 1937.

ARANHA, José Pereira da Graça (Brazil 1868–1931)

Canaan – Fiction. Trans. Mariano Joaquim Lorente. Four Seas Co: Boston, 1920; Allen & Unwin: London, 1921. *Canaã*, 1902.

ARENAL, Humberto (Cuba 1927–)

The Sun Beats Down, a Novella of the Cuban Revolution – Fiction. Trans. J. S. Bernstein. Hill & Wang: New York, 1959. *El sol a plomo*, 1958.

ARENAS, Reinaldo (Cuba 1943–)

Hallucinations: Being an Account of the Life and Adventures of Friar Servando Teresa de Mier – Fiction. Trans. Gordon Brotherston. Harper & Row: New York, 1971; Cape: London, 1971; Penguin Books: Harmondsworth, 1972. *El mundo alucinante*, 1969.

El Central – Poetry. Avon Books: New York, 1983. *El central*, 1981.

Farewell to the Sea: a Novel of Cuba – Fiction. Trans. Andrew Hurley. Viking: New York, 1986; Penguin: New York, 1988. *Otra vez, el mar*, 1982.

Graveyard of the Angels – Fiction. Trans. Alfred J. MacAdam. Avon Books: New York, 1987. Title and date of original unknown.

The Ill-Fated Peregrinations of Fray Servando – Fiction. Trans. Andrew Hurley. Avon Books: New York, 1987. *El mundo alucinante*, 1969.

Singing from the Well – Fiction. Viking: New York, 1987. *Celestino antes del alba*, 1980.

ARGUEDAS, José María (Peru 1911–69)

The Singing Mountains: Songs and Tales of the Quechua People – Poetry. Trans. & ed. Ruth Stephan. Univ. of Texas Press: Austin, 1971. *Canto Kechwa*, 1938.

Deep Rivers – Fiction. Trans. Frances H. Barraclough. Introd. John Murra. Afterword Mario Vargas Llosa. Univ. of Texas Press: Austin, 1978. *Los ríos profundos*, 1958.

Yawar Fiesta – Fiction. Trans. Frances H. Barraclough. Univ. of Texas Press: Austin, 1984; Quartet: London, 1985. *Yawar Fiesta*, 1941.

ARGUETA, Manlio (El Salvador 1935–)

One Day of Life – Fiction. Trans. Bill Brow. Chatto & Windus: London, 1984; Aventura: New York, 1985. *Un día en la vida*, 1980.

Cuzcatlán – Fiction. Trans. Clark Hansen. Chatto & Windus: London, 1987; Aventura: New York, 1987. *Cuzcatlán, donde bate la mar del sur*, 1986.

ARIDJIS, Homero (Mexico 1940–)

Los espacios azules. Blue Spaces; Selected Poems of Homero Aridjis – Poetry. Ed. & introd. Kenneth Rexroth. Trans. Kenneth Rexroth, W. S. Merwin, Eliot Weinberger, Nathaniel Tarn, Michael Schmidt. Seabury Press: New York, 1974.

Exaltation of Light – Poetry. Bilingual. Ed. & trans. Eliot Weinberger. Boa Editions: Brockport, NY, 1981. *Quemar las naves*, 1975 and *Vivir para ver*, 1977.

ARLT, Roberto (Argentina 1900–42)

The Seven Madmen – Fiction. Trans. Naomi Lindstrom. Godine: Boston, 1984. *Los siete locos*, 1929.

ARMAND, Octavio (Cuba 1946–)

With Dusk – Poetry. Trans. Carol Maier. Logbridge-Rhodes: Durango, Colo., 1984.

ARREOLA, Juan José (Mexico 1918–)

Confabulario and Other Inventions – Fiction. Trans. George D. Schade. Univ. of Texas Press: Austin, 1964. *Confabulario total*, 1962.

The Fair – Fiction. Trans. John Upton. Univ. of Texas Press: Austin, 1977. *La feria*, 1963.

ASTRADA, Etelvina (Argentina 1930–)

Autobiography at the Trigger – Poetry. Trans. Timothy Rogers. Spanish Literature: York, SC, 1983. *Autobiografía con gatillo*, 1980.

ASTURIAS, Miguel Angel (Guatemala 1899–1974)

The President – Fiction. Trans. Frances Partridge. Gollancz: London, 1963; publ. as *El señor presidente*, Atheneum: New York, 1969. *El señor presidente*, 1946.

Mulata – Fiction. Trans. Gregory Rabassa. Delacorte Press: New York, 1967; publ. as *The Mulata and Mister Fly*, Peter Owen: London, 1967; Penguin Books: Harmondsworth, 1970. *Mulata de tal*, 1963.

The Cyclone – Fiction. Trans. Darwin J. Flakoll and Claribel Alegría. Peter Owen: London, 1967. *Viento fuerte*, 1950.

Strong Wind – Fiction. Trans. Gregory Rabassa. Delacorte Press: New York, 1969. *Viento fuerte*, 1950.

The Green Pope – Fiction. Trans. Gregory Rabassa. Delacorte Press: New York, 1971; Cape: London, 1971. *El papa verde*, 1954.

The Bejewelled Boy – Fiction. Trans. Martin Shuttleworth. Doubleday: New York, 1971. *El alhajadito*, 1961.

The Talking Machine – Fiction. Trans. Beverly Koch. Doubleday: New York, 1971. One story from *El alhajadito*, 1961.

The Eyes of the Interred – Fiction. Trans. Gregory Rabassa. Delacorte Press: St. Lawrence, NY, 1972; Cape: London, 1974. *Los ojos de los enterrados*, 1960.

Men of Maize – Fiction. Trans. Gerald Martin. Delacorte Press: St. Lawrence, NY, 1975; Verso: London, 1988. *Hombres de maíz*, 1949.

Guatemalan Sociology – Essay. Trans. Maureen Ahern. Arizona State Univ. Press: Tempe, 1977. *Sociología guatemalteca*, date unknown.

AZEVEDO, Aluízio de (Brazil 1857–1913)

A Brazilian Tenement – Fiction. Trans. Harry W. Brown. McBride & Co: New York, 1926; Cassell: London, 1928; Howard Fertig: New York, 1976. *O cortiço*, 1890.

AZUELA, Arturo (Mexico 1938–)

Shadows of Silence – Fiction. Trans. Elena C. Murray. Univ. of Notre Dame Press: Notre Dame, Ind., 1985. *Manifestación de silencios*, 1979.

AZUELA, Mariano (Mexico 1873–1952)

The Underdogs, a Novel of the Mexican Revolution – Fiction. Trans. Enrique Munguía. Brentano's: New York, 1929; Cape: London, 1930; New American Library: New York, 1963. *Los de abajo*, 1916.

Marcela, a Mexican Love Story – Fiction. Trans. Anita Brenner. Farrar & Rinehart: New York, 1932. *Mala yerba*, 1909.

Two Novels of Mexico: The Flies and the Bosses – Fiction. Trans. Lesley Byrd Simpson. Univ. of California Press: Berkeley & Los Angeles, 1956; Cambridge Univ. Press: Cambridge, 1956. *Las moscas*, 1918 and *Los caciques*, 1917.

Three Novels: The Trials of a Respectable Family; The Underdogs; The Firefly – Fiction. Trans. Frances K. Hendricks and Beatrice Berler. Trinity Univ. Press: San Antonio, Tex., 1963; 1979. *Las tribulaciones de una familia decente*, 1919; *Los de abajo*, 1916 and *La luciérnaga*, 1932.

The Underdogs, in *Azuela and the Mexican Underdogs*. Trans. Stanley L. Robe. Univ. of California Press: Berkeley, 1979. *Los de abajo*, 1916.

B

BANDEIRA, Manuel (Brazil 1886–1968)

A Brief History of Brazilian Literature – Essay. Trans. Charles Frank. Publishers: New York, 1964. *Noções da história das literaturas*, 1938.

Recife – Poetry. Trans. Eddie Flintoff. Rivelin Grapheme Press: Bradford, 1984.

This Earth, That Sky: Poems by Manuel Bandeira – Poetry. Trans. Candace Slater. Univ. of California Press: Berkeley, 1988.

BARRIOS, Eduardo (Chile 1884–1963)

Brother Asno – Fiction. Trans. Edmundo García Girón. Las Américas: New York, 1969. *El hermano asno*, 1922.

BELLI, Gioconda (Nicaragua 1948–)

From Eve's Rib – Poetry. Bilingual. Trans. Steven F. White. Curbstone Press: Willimantic, Conn., 1989. *Línea de fuego*, 1978.

Nicaragua under Fire – Poetry. Trans. John Lyon. Warwick: Greville: London, 1989.

BENEDETTI, Mario (Uruguay 1920–)

The Truce – Fiction. Trans. Benjamin Graham. Harper & Row: New York, 1969. *La tregua*, 1960.

BENÍTEZ, Fernando (Mexico 1912–)

The Poisoned Water – Fiction. Trans. Mary Ellsworth. Southern Illinois Univ. Press: Carbondale, 1973. *El agua envenenada*, 1961.

In the Magic Land of Peyote – Essay. Trans. John Upton. Introd. Peter

Furst. Univ. of Texas Press: Austin, 1975. *En la tierra mágica del peyote*, 1971.

BIANCO, José (Argentina 1909–84)

Shadow Play and *The Rats* – Fiction. Trans. Daniel Balderston. Latin American Literary Review Press: Pittsburgh, 1984. *Sombras suele vestir*, 1941 and *Las ratas*, 1943.

BIOY CASARES, Adolfo (Argentina 1914–)

The Invention of Morel and Other Stories – Fiction. Trans. Ruth L. C. Simms. Prol. Jorge Luis Borges. Univ. of Texas Press: Austin, 1961. *La invención de Morel*, 1940 and *La trama celeste*, 1948.

Diary of the War of the Pig – Fiction. Trans. Gregory Woodruff and Donald Yates. McGraw-Hill: New York, 1972. *Diario de la guerra del cerdo*, 1969.

A Plan for Escape – Fiction. Trans. Suzanne Jill Levine. Dutton: New York, 1975; Graywolf Press: St. Paul's, Minn., 1988. *Plan de evasión*, 1945.

Asleep in the Sun – Fiction. Trans. Suzanne Jill Levine. Persea Books: New York, 1978. *Dormir al sol*, 1973.

The Dream of the Hero – Fiction. Trans. Diana Thorold. Quartet: London, 1987. *El sueño de los héroes*, 1954.

see also items under Jorge Luis **Borges**.

BLANCO FOMBONA, Rufino (Venezuela 1874–1944)

The Man of Gold – Fiction. Trans. Isaac Goldberg. Brentano's: New York, 1920. *El hombre de oro*, 1915.

BLEST GANA, Alberto (Chile 1830–1920)

Martín Rivas – Fiction. Trans. Mrs. Charles Whithan. Chapman & Hall: London, 1916; Knopf: New York, 1918; Gordon Press: New York, 1977. *Martín Rivas*, 1862.

BOMBAL, María Luisa (Chile 1910–80)

The House of Mist – Fiction. Trans. by author. Farrar, Straus: New York, 1947. *La última niebla*, 1935.

The Shrouded Woman – Fiction. Trans. by author. Farrar, Straus: New York, 1948. *La amortajada*, 1938.

New Islands and Other Stories – Fiction. Trans. Richard and Lucía Cunningham. Preface Jorge Luis Borges. Farrar, Straus & Giroux: New York, 1982; Cornell Univ. Press: Ithaca, NY, 1988. *Trenzas* and *La última niebla*, 1935.

BORGE MARTÍNEZ, Tomás (Nicaragua 1930–)

Christianity and Revolution, Tomás Borge's Theology of Life – Essay. Ed. & trans. Andrew Reding. Orbis Books: New York, 1987.

Have You Seen a Red Curtain in My Weary Chamber? – Fiction/poetry/essay. Ed. & trans. Russell Bartley, Kent Johnson and Sylvia Yoneda. Curbstone Press: Willimantic, Conn., 1989.

BORGES, Jorge Luis (Argentina 1899–1986)

Labyrinths: Selected Stories and Other Writings – Fiction. Ed. Donald Yates and James E. Irby. Trans. editors and John Fein, Dudley Fitts, Julian Palley and others. New Directions: New York, 1962; Penguin Books: Harmondsworth, 1970.

Ficciones – Fiction. Trans. Anthony Kerrigan, Alastair Reid and others. Grove Press: New York, 1962; Weidenfeld & Nicolson: London, 1962; publ. as *Fictions*, Calder: London, 1965. *Ficciones*, 1944 and 1956.

Other Inquisitions – Essays. Trans. Ruth L. C. Simms. Introd. James E. Irby. Univ. of Texas Press: Austin, 1964; Simon & Schuster: New York, 1965; Washington Square Press: New York, 1966; Souvenir Press: London, 1973. *Otras inquisiciones*, 1952.

Dreamtigers – Poetry. Trans. Mildred Boyer and Harold Morland. Introd. Miguel Enguidanos. Univ. of Texas Press: Austin, 1964; Souvenir Press: London, 1973. *El hacedor*, 1960.

A Personal Anthology. Trans. & ed. Anthony Kerrigan. Trans. Elaine Kerrigan, Alastair Reid and Irving Feldman. Grove Press: New York, 1967; Cape: London, 1968; Picador: London, 1972. *Antología personal*, 1961.

The Book of Imaginary Beings, with Margarita Guerrero – Essay/Fiction. Trans. Norman Thomas di Giovanni in collab. with the author. Dutton: New York, 1969; Cape: London, 1970; Avon Books: New York, 1970; Penguin Books: Harmondsworth, 1984. *El libro de los seres imaginarios*, 1967, an enlargement of *Manual de zoología fantástica*, 1957.

The Aleph and Other Stories, 1933-1969 – Fiction. Trans. & ed. Norman Thomas di Giovanni in collab. with the author. Dutton: New York, 1970; Cape: London, 1971; Picador: London, 1973.

Extraordinary Tales, with Adolfo Bioy Casares – Fiction. Trans. & ed. Anthony Kerrigan. Herder & Herder: New York, 1971; Souvenir Press: London, 1973. *Cuentos breves y extraordinarios*, 1967.

An Introduction to American Literature, with Esther Zemborain de Torres – Essay. Trans. & ed. L. Clark Keating and Robert O. Evans. Univ. of Kentucky Press: Kentucky, 1971; Schoken: New York, 1973. *Introducción a la literatura norteamericana*, 1967.

Selected Poems (1923–1967) – Poetry. Bilingual. Ed. with introd. & notes Norman Thomas di Giovanni. Trans. di Giovanni, Alastair Reid, John Hollander, Richard Wilbur, W. S. Merwin, Richard Howard and others. Delacorte Press: New York, 1972; Allen Lane: Harmondsworth, 1972; Penguin Books: Harmondsworth, 1985.

A Universal History of Infamy – Fiction. Trans. Norman Thomas di Giovanni. Dutton: New York, 1972; Allen Lane: London, 1973; Penguin Books: Harmondsworth, 1975. *Historia universal de la infamia*, 1935 and 1954.

Doctor Brodie's Report – Fiction. Trans. Norman Thomas di Giovanni, in collab. with the author. Dutton: New York, 1972; Bantam: New York, 1973; Allen Lane: Harmondsworth, 1974; Penguin Books: Harmondsworth, 1976. *El informe de Brodie*, 1970.

The Congress – Fiction. Trans. Norman Thomas di Giovanni. Enitharmon Press: London, 1973. *El congreso*, 1971.

In Praise of Darkness – Poetry. Bilingual. Trans. Norman Thomas di Giovanni. Dutton: New York, 1974; Allen Lane: London, 1975. *Elogio de la sombra*, 1969.

Introduction to English Literature, with María Esther Vázquez–Essay. Trans. L. C. Keating and R. O. Evans. Robson Books: London, 1975.

Chronicles of Bustos Domecq, with Adolfo Bioy Casares – Fiction. Trans. Norman Thomas di Giovanni. Dutton: New York, 1976; Allen Lane: London, 1982. *Crónicas de Bustos Domecq*, 1967.

The Gold of the Tigers. Selected Later Poems – Poetry. Bilingual. Trans. Alastair Reid. Dutton: New York, 1977. *El oro de los tigres*, 1972 and *La rosa profunda*, 1975.

The Book of Sand – Fiction. Trans. Norman Thomas di Giovanni. Dutton: New York, 1977; Allen Lane: London, 1979; Penguin Books:

Harmondsworth, 1979. British edition includes *The Gold of the Tigers* (poetry). *El libro de arena*, 1975.

Six Problems for Don Isidro Parodi, with Adolfo Bioy Casares – Fiction. Trans. Norman Thomas di Giovanni. Dutton: New York, 1981; Allen Lane: London, 1981. *Seis problemas para don Isidro Parodi*, 1942.

Borges. A Reader. A Selection from the Writings of Jorge Luis Borges. Eds. Emir Rodríguez Monegal and Alastair Reid. Trans. include Norman Thomas di Giovanni, Alastair Reid, Ben Belitt, Suzanne Jill Levine, Karen Stolley, Anthony Kerrigan, Ruth Simms. Dutton: New York, 1981.

Evaristo Carriego – Essay. Trans. Norman Thomas di Giovanni. Dutton: New York, 1984. *Evaristo Carriego*, 1930 and 1955.

Seven Nights – Essay. Trans. Eliot Weinberger. New Directions: New York, 1984; Faber & Faber: London, 1986. *Siete noches*, 1980.

Atlas, in collab. with María Kodama – Essay. Trans. Anthony Kerrigan. Dutton: New York, 1985; Viking: London, 1986. *Atlas*, 1984.

BRANDÃO, Ignácio de Loyola (Brazil 1936–)

Zero – Fiction. Trans. Ellen Watson. Avon Books: New York, 1984. *Zero*, 1975.

And Still the Earth – Fiction. 1985 (other publication details unknown). *Não verás país nenhum*, 1981.

C

CABRERA INFANTE, Guillermo (Cuba 1929–)

Three Trapped Tigers – Fiction. Trans. Donald Gardner and Suzanne Jill Levine, with the author. Harper & Row: New York, 1971; Picador: London, 1980; Faber & Faber: London, 1989. *Tres tristes tigres*, 1965.

View of the Dawn in the Tropics – Essay. Trans. Suzanne Jill Levine. Harper & Row: New York, 1978; Faber & Faber: London, 1988. *Vista del amanecer en el trópico*, 1974.

Infante's Inferno – Fiction. Trans. Suzanne Jill Levine and author. Harper & Row: New York, 1984; Faber & Faber: London, 1984. *La Habana para un infante difunto*, 1979.

Holy Smoke – Essay. Written in English. Faber & Faber: London, 1985; Harper & Row: New York, 1986.

CALLADO, Antônio (Brazil 1917–)

Quarup – Fiction. Trans. Barbara Shelby. Knopf: New York, 1970. *Quarup*, 1967.

Don Juan's Bar – Fiction. Trans. Barbara Shelby. Knopf: New York, 1972. *Bar Don Juan*, 1971.

CAMPOBELLO, Nellie (Mexico 1912–)

Cartucho and My Mother's Hands – Fiction. Trans. Doris Meyer and Irene Matthews. Introd. Elena Poniatowska. Univ. of Texas Press: Austin, 1988. *Cartucho; relatos de la lucha en el norte de México*, 1931.

CANTÓN, Darío (Argentina 1928–)

Poamorio – Poetry. Trans. Drew McCord Stroud. Introd. Jean Franco. Saru Publications: Sedona, Ariz., 1984.

CARBALLIDO, Emilio (Mexico 1925–)

The Norther (El norte) – Fiction. Trans. Margaret Sayers Peden. Univ. of Texas Press: Austin, 1968. *El norte*, 1958.

The Golden Thread and Other Plays – Theatre. Trans. Margaret Sayers Peden. Univ. of Texas Press: Austin, 1970. *La hebra de oro*, 1956; *La triple porfía*, 1948; *El lugar y la hora*, 1956; *Teseo*, 1962; *El relojero de Córdoba*, 1960.

CARDENAL, Ernesto (Nicaragua 1925–)

The Psalms of Struggle and Liberation – Poetry. Trans. Emile G. McAnany. Foreword Thomas Merton. Herder & Herder: New York, 1971; Seabury Press: New York, 1973. *Salmos*, 1964.

To Live is to Love – Essay. Trans. Kurt Reinhardt. Herder & Herder: New York, 1972; Doubleday: Garden City, NY, 1974. *Vida en el amor*, 1970.

Homage to the American Indians – Poetry. Trans. Monique and Carlos Altschul. Johns Hopkins Univ. Press: Baltimore, 1973. *Homenaje a los indios americanos*, 1969.

In Cuba – Essay. Trans. Donald Walsh. New Directions: New York, 1974. *En Cuba*, 1970.

Love. Vida en el amor – Essay. Trans. Dinah Livingstone. Search Press: London, 1974; Crossroads: New York, 1981. *Vida en el amor*, 1970.

Marilyn Monroe and other Poems – Poetry. Trans. & introd. Robert Pring-Mill. Search Press: London, 1975. *Oración por Marilyn Monroe y otros poemas*, 1965.

Apocalypse and Other Poems – Poetry. Sel. & ed. Robert Pring-Mill and Donald Walsh. Introd. R. Pring-Mill. Trans. Robert Pring-Mill, Donald Walsh, Thomas Merton, Kenneth Rexroth, Mireya Jaimes Freyre. New Directions: New York, 1977.

Gospel in Solentiname – Essay. Trans. Donald Walsh. Vols. 1 to 4. Orbis Books: New York, 1978–82; Search Press: London, 1977 (vol. 1). *El evangelio en Solentiname*, 1975–77.

Epigramas – Poetry. Trans. K. H. Anton. Lodestar Press: New York, 1978. *Epigramas*, 1961.

Zero Hour and other Documentary Poems – Poetry. Sel. & ed. Donald Walsh. Introd. Robert Pring-Mill. Trans. Donald Walsh, Robert Pring-Mill, Paul Borgeson Jr., Jonathan Cohen. New Directions: New York, 1980.

Psalms – Poetry. Trans. Thomas Blackburn, John Heath-Stubbs, Elizabeth Jennings, Tony Rudolf, Peter Levi, John Griffiths. Sheed & Ward: London, 1981; Crossroads: New York, 1981. *Salmos*, 1964.

With Walker in Nicaragua and Other Early Poems, 1949–1954 – Poetry. Bilingual. Trans. & sel. Jonathan Cohen. Wesleyan Univ. Press: Middletown, Conn., 1984.

Flights of Victory. Vuelo de victoria – Poetry. Bilingual. Trans., ed. & introd. Marc Zimmerman. Orbis Books: New York, 1985; Curbstone Press: Willimantic, Conn., 1988.

From Nicaragua with Love. Poems 1979–1986 – Poetry. Trans. & introd. Jonathan Cohen. City Lights: San Francisco, 1986.

Nicaraguan New Time – Poetry. Trans. Dinah Livingstone. Journeyman: London, 1988.

CARNEIRO, Cecilio (Brazil 1911–)

The Bonfire – Fiction. Trans. Dudly Poore. Greenwood Press: Westport Conn., 1972. *A fogueira*, 1939.

CARPENTIER, Alejo (Cuba 1904–79)

The Lost Steps – Fiction. Trans. Harriet de Onís. Knopf: New York, 1956; Gollancz: London, 1956; Penguin Books: Harmondsworth, 1968. *Los pasos perdidos*, 1953.

The Kingdom of this World – Fiction. Trans. Harriet de Onís. Knopf: New York, 1957; Gollancz: London, 1967; Penguin Books: Harmondsworth, 1975. *El reino de este mundo*, 1949.

Explosion in a Cathedral – Fiction. Trans. John Sturrock. Gollancz: London, 1963; Little Brown: Boston, 1963; Penguin Books: Harmondsworth, 1971. *El siglo de las luces*, 1962.

War on Time – Fiction. Trans. Frances Partridge. Knopf: New York, 1969; Gollancz: London, 1970. *Guerra del tiempo*, 1956.

Reasons of State – Fiction. Trans. Frances Partridge. Gollancz: London, 1976; Knopf: New York, 1976; Writers & Readers Publ. Coop.: London, 1977. *Recurso del método*, 1974.

Concierto barroco – Fiction. Trans. Asa Zatz. Council Oak Books: Tulsa, Okla., 1988. *Concierto barroco*, 1974.

CARRERA ANDRADE, Jorge (Ecuador 1903–78)

To the Bay Bridge – Poetry. Trans. Eleanor L. Turnbull. Stanford Univ. Press: Stanford, Calif., 1941. *Canto al puente de Oakland*, 1941.

Secret Country – Poetry. Trans. Muna Lee. Macmillan: New York, 1946. *País secreto*, 1940.

Visitor of Mist – Poetry. Trans. G. R. Coulthard and K. Nott. Williams & Norgate: London, 1950. *El visitante de niebla*, 1947.

Selected Poems of Jorge Carrera Andrade – Poetry. Bilingual. Ed. & trans, H. R. Hays. State Univ. of New York: Albany, 1972.

Reflections on Spanish American Poetry – Essay. Trans. D. C. Bliss and Gabriela de Bliss. State Univ. of New York: Albany, 1973.

CASTELLANOS, Rosario (Mexico 1925–74)

The Nine Guardians – Fiction. Trans. Irene Nicholson. Faber & Faber: London, 1959; Vanguard: New York, 1960. *Balún-Canán*, 1957.

Looking at the Mona Lisa – Poetry. Trans. Maureen Ahern. Rivelin/ Equatorial: Bradford, 1981.

Meditation on the Threshold: A Bilingual Anthology of Poetry – Poetry. Bilingual. Trans. & introd. Julian Palley. Bilingual Review Press: Tempe, Ariz., 1988.

A Rosario Castellanos Reader – Poetry, essay, fiction, theatre. Trans. & ed. with introd. Maureen Ahern, with others. Univ. of Texas Press: Austin, 1988.

The Selected Poems of Rosario Castellanos – Poetry. Trans. Magda Bogin. Introd. Elena Poniatowska. Graywolf Press: St. Paul's, Minn., 1988.

CASTILLO, Otto René (Guatemala 1936–67)

Let's Go! – Poetry. Bilingual. Trans. with introd. Margaret Randall. Cape Goliard Press: London, 1971; Curbstone Press: Willimantic, Conn., 1984. *Vámonos patria a caminar*, 1965.

Tomorrow Triumphant. Selected Poems – Poetry. Trans. Roque Dalton Cultural Brigade. Ed. Magaly Fernandez and David Volpendesta. Night Horn Books: San Francisco, 1984.

CHOCANO, José Santos (Peru 1875–1934)

Spirit of the Andes – Poetry. Trans. Edna Worthley Underwood. The Mosher Press: Portland, Ore., 1935.

CISNEROS, Antonio (Peru 1942–)

The Spider Hangs too far from the Ground – Poetry. Trans. Maureen Ahern, William Rowe and David Tipton. Cape: London, 1970.

Helicopters in the Kingdom of Peru – Poetry. Trans. Maureen Ahern, William Rowe and David Tipton. Rivelin/Equatorial: Bradford, 1981.

At Night the Cats – Poetry. Bilingual. Trans. Maureen Ahern, William Rowe and David Tipton. Red Dust: New York, 1985.

Land of Angels – Poetry. Trans. Maureen Ahern, William Rowe and David Tipton. Aquila: Isle of Skye, 1985.

CONSTANTINI, Humberto (Argentina 1924–87)

Of Gods, Little Men and Police – Fiction. Trans. Toby Talbot. Harper & Row: New York, 1984. *De dioses, hombrecitos y policías*, 1979.

The Long Night of Francisco Sanctis – Fiction. Trans. Norman Thomas di Giovanni. Harper & Row: New York, 1985; Fontana: London, 1987. *La larga noche de Francisco Sanctis*, 1984.

CORÇÃO, Gustavo (Brazil 1896–1978)

My Neighbour as Myself – Fiction. Trans. Clotilde Wilson. Longmans Green: London, 1957. *A descoberta do outro*, 1944.

Who if I Cry Out – Fiction. Trans. Clotilde Wilson. Univ. of Texas Press: Austin, 1967. *Lições de abismo*, 1950.

CORTÁZAR, Julio (Argentina 1914–84)

The Winners – Fiction. Trans. Elaine Kerrigan. Pantheon Books: New York, 1965; Allison & Busby: London, 1968. *Los premios*, 1960.

Hopscotch – Fiction. Trans. Gregory Rabassa. Pantheon Books: New York, 1966; Collins: London, 1967; Avon Books: New York, 1974. *Rayuela*, 1963.

End of the Game and Other Stories – Fiction. Trans. Paul Blackburn. Pantheon Books: New York, 1967; Collins & Harvill: London, 1968 (also

Blow-up and Other Stories). *Bestiario*, 1951, *Final del juego*, 1956 and *Las armas secretas*, 1959.

Cronopios and Famas – Fiction. Trans. Paul Blackburn. Pantheon Books: New York, 1969; Marion Boyars: London, 1976. *Historia de cronopios y famas*, 1962.

All Fires the Fire, and Other Stories – Fiction. Trans. Suzanne Jill Levine. Marion Boyars: London, 1971; Pantheon Books: New York, 1973. *Todos los fuegos el fuego*, 1966.

62: A Model Kit – Fiction. Trans. Gregory Rabassa. Pantheon Books: New York, 1972; Marion Boyars: London, 1977. *62: modelo para armar*, 1968.

A Manual for Manuel – Fiction. Trans. Gregory Rabassa. Pantheon Books: New York, 1978; Harvill Press: London, 1984. *Libro de Manuel*, 1973.

A Change of Light and Other Stories – Fiction. Trans. Gregory Rabassa. Knopf: New York, 1980; Harvill Press: London, 1984; Arena: London, 1987. *Alguien que anda por ahí*, 1977.

We Love Glenda so Much and Other Tales – Fiction. Trans. Gregory Rabassa. Knopf: New York, 1983; Harvill Press: London, 1984. *Queremos tanto a Glenda*, 1981.

A Certain Lucas – Fiction. Trans. Gregory Rabassa. Knopf: New York, 1984. *Un tal Lucas*, 1979.

Around the Day in Eighty Worlds – Fiction & essay. Trans. Thomas Christensen. North Point Press: San Francisco, 1986. *La vuelta al día en ochenta mundos*, 1967.

CRUZ, Sor Juana Inés de la (Mexico 1648–94)

The Pathless Grove: Sonnets – Poetry. Trans. Pauline Cook. Decker Press: Prairie City, Ill., 1950.

Woman of Genius, the Intellectual Autobiography of Sor Juana Inés de la Cruz. Trans. Margaret Sayers Peden. Lime Rock Press: Salisbury, Conn., 1982. *Respuesta a sor Filotea de la Cruz, 1690*.

Poems. Trans. Margaret Sayers Peden. Bilingual Press: Binghampton, NY, 1985.

Sor Juana's Dream – Poetry. Bilingual. Trans., introd. & commentary Luis Harss. Lumen Books: New York, 1986.

A Sor Juana Anthology – Poetry. Trans. Alan S. Trueblood. Foreword Octavio Paz. Harvard Univ. Press: Cambridge, Mass., 1988.

CUADRA, Pablo Antonio (Nicaragua 1912–)

The Jaguar and the Moon – Poetry. Trans. Thomas Merton. Unicorn Press: Greensboro, NC, 1972.

Songs of Cifar and the Sweet Sea. Selections 1967–1977 – Poetry. Trans. Grace Schulman and Ann McCarthy de Zavala. Columbia Univ. Press: New York, 1979.

The Birth of the Sun: Selected Poems 1935–1985 – Poetry. Trans. & ed. Steven F. White. Unicorn Press: Greensboro, NC, 1988.

CUZA MALÉ, Belkis (Cuba 1942–)

Belkis Cuza Malé: Woman in the Front Lines – Poetry. Bilingual. Trans. Pamela Carmell. Unicorn Press: Greensboro, NC, 1988.

D

DALTON, Roque (El Salvador 1935–75)

Poems – Poetry. Trans. Richard Schaaf. Curbstone Press: Willimantic, Conn., 1984. *La ventana en el rostro*, 1961; *El turno del ofendido*, 1963; *Taberna y otros lugares*, 1969; *Las historias prohibidas del pulgarcito*, 1974 and *Poemas clandestinos*, 1976.

Poemas clandestinos / Clandestine Poems – Poetry. Trans. Jack Hirschman. Introd. Margaret Randall. Solidarity Publications: San Francisco, 1984. *Poemas clandestinos*, 1976.

Miguel Mármol – Fiction. Trans. Kathleen Ross and Richard Schaaf. Introd. Manlio Argueta. Curbstone Press: Willimantic, Conn., 1986. *Miguel Mármol*, 1982.

Poesía militante/ Militant Poetry – Poetry. Trans. Arlene and James Scully. El Salvador Cultural Commission: London, date not stated.

DARÍO, Rubén – pseud. for Félix Rubén García Sarmiento (Nicaragua 1867-1916)

Prosas profanas and other Poems – Poetry. Trans. Charles McMichael. N. L. Brown: New York, 1922. *Prosas profanas*, 1896.

Selected Poems – Poetry. Trans. Lysander Kemp. Introd. Octavio Paz. Univ. of Texas Press: Austin, 1965.

del PASO, Fernando (Mexico 1935–)

Palinuro of Mexico – Fiction. Trans. Elizabeth Plaister. Quartet: London, 1989. *Palinuro de México*, 1977.

DENEVI, Marco (Argentina 1922–)

Rosa at Ten O'clock – Fiction. Trans. Donald Yates. Holt, Rinehart & Winston: New York, 1964. *Rosaura a las diez*, 1955.

DESNOES, Edmundo (Cuba 1930–)

Inconsolable Memories – Fiction. Trans. by author. New York, 1967; André Deutsch: London, 1968; publ. as *Memories of Underdevelopment*, Penguin Books: Harmondsworth, 1971. *Memorias del subdesarrollo*, 1965.

DÍAZ SÁNCHEZ, Ramón (Venezuela 1903–68)

Cumboto – Fiction. Trans. John Upton. Univ. of Texas Press: Austin, 1969. *Cumboto; cuento de siete leguas*, 1950.

DÍAZ VALCARCEL, Emilio (Puerto Rico 1925–)

Schemes in the Month of March – Fiction. Trans. Nancy Sebastiani. Bilingual Review Press: Ypsilanti, Mich., 1980. *Figuraciones en el mes de marzo*, 1972.

DONOSO, José (Chile 1924–)

Coronation – Fiction. Trans. Jocasta Goodwin. Knopf: New York, 1965; Bodley Head: London, 1965. *Coronación*, 1957.

This Sunday – Fiction. Trans. Lorraine O'Grady Freeman. Knopf: New York, 1967; Bodley Head: London, 1968. *Este domingo*, 1965.

The Obscene Bird of Night – Fiction. Trans. Hardie St. Martin and Leonard Mades. Knopf: New York, 1973; Cape: London, 1974. *El obsceno pájaro de la noche*, 1970.

Hell has No Limits, in *Triple Cross* – Fiction. Trans. Suzanne Jill Levine. Dutton: New York, 1973. *El lugar sin límites*, 1966.

The Boom in Spanish American Literature: a Personal History – Essay. Trans. Gregory Kolovakos. Columbia Univ. Press & Center for Inter-American Relations: New York, 1977. *Historia personal del 'boom'*, 1972.

Sacred Families: Three Novellas – Fiction. Trans. Andrée Conrad. Knopf: New York, 1977; Gollancz: London, 1978. *Tres novelitas burguesas*, 1973.

Charleston and Other Stories – Fiction. Trans. Andrée Conrad. Godine: Boston, 1977. *Cuentos*, 1971.

A House in the Country – Fiction. Trans. David Pritchard, with Suzanne Jill Levine. Knopf: New York, 1983; Allen Lane: London, 1984. *Casa de campo*, 1978.

Curfew – Fiction. Trans. Alfred MacAdam. Weidenfeld & Nicolson: New York, 1988. *La desesperanza*, 1986.

DORFMAN, Ariel (Argentina/Chile 1942–)

Widows – Fiction. Trans. Stephen Kessler. Random House: New York, 1983; Pluto Press: London, 1984; Viking Penguin: New York, 1989. *Viudas*, 1981.

The Empire's Old Clothes: What the Lone Ranger, Babar and other Innocent Heroes do to our Minds – Essay. Trans. Clark Hansen. Pantheon: New York, 1983; Pluto Press: London, 1983.

How to Read Donald Duck: Imperialist Ideology in the Disney Comic, with Armand Mattelart – Essay. International General: New York, 1984. *Para leer a Pato Donald*, 1971.

The Last Song of Manuel Sendero – Fiction. Trans. George R. Shivers, with the author. Viking: New York, 1987. *La última canción de Manuel Sendero*, 1982.

Last Waltz in Santiago and other Poems of Exile and Disappearance – Poetry. Trans. Edith Grossman, with the author. Viking Penguin: New York, 1988.

Mascara – Fiction. Written in English. Viking Penguin: New York, 1988.

DOURADO, Autran (Brazil 1926–)

A Hidden Life – Fiction. Trans. Edgar Miller Jr. Knopf: New York, 1969. *Uma vida en segrêdo*, 1964.

The Voices of the Dead – Fiction. Trans. John Parker. Peter Owen: London, 1980; Tapingler: New York, 1981. *Opera dos mortos*, 1967.

Pattern for a Tapestry – Fiction. Trans. John Parker. Peter Owen: London, 1984. *O risco do bordado*, 1970.

The Bells of Agony – Fiction. Trans. John Parker. Peter Owen: London, 1988. *Os sinos da agonia*, 1974.

DRUMMOND de ANDRADE, Carlos (Brazil 1902–87)

In the Middle of the Road. Selected Poems – Poetry. Bilingual. Trans. & ed. John Nist. Univ. of Arizona Press: Tucson, 1965.

The Minus Sign. A Selection from the Poetic Anthology – Poetry. Trans. Virginia de Araujo. Black Swan Press: Chicago, 1980; Carcanet: Manchester, 1981.

Travelling in the Family: Selected Poems – Poetry. Eds. Thomas Colchie and Mark Strand. Trans. Thomas Colchie, Mark Strand, Elizabeth Bishop and Gregory Rabassa. Random House: New York, 1986.

E

ECHEVERRÍA, Esteban (Argentina 1805–51)

The Slaughter House – Fiction. Trans. Angel Flores. Las Américas: New York, 1959. *El matadero*, 1871.

EDWARDS, Jorge (Chile 1931–)

Persona Non Grata. An Envoy in Castro's Cuba – Fiction. Trans. Colin Harding. Bodley Head: London, 1976. Pomerica Press: New York, 1977. *Persona non grata*, 1973.

ETCHEVERRY, Jorge (Chile 1948–)

The Escape Artist. Poems 1968–1980 – Poetry. Bilingual. Trans. Christina Shantz. Ediciones Cordillera: Ottawa, 1981.

F

FERNÁNDEZ, Macedonio (Argentina 1874–1952)

Macedonio: Selected Writings in Translation – Essay & Fiction. Ed. Jo Anne Engelbert. Trans. Jo Anne Englebert, William Chamurro, Edith Grossman, Peter Hulme, Naomi Lindstrom, Paula Speck, Gregory Kolovakos. Latitudes Press: Fort Worth, Tex., 1984.

FERNÁNDEZ de LIZARDI, José Joaquín (Mexico 1776–1827)

The Itching Parrot – Fiction. Trans. Katherine Anne Porter. Doubleday: Garden City, NY, 1942. *El periquillo sarniento*, 1816.

FONSECA, Rubem (Brazil 1925–)

High Art – Fiction. Trans. Ellen Watson. Harper & Row: New York, 1986; Carrol & Graf: New York, 1987. *A grande arte*, 1983.

FRAILE, Isabel (Mexico 1934–)

Isabel Fraile: Poems – Poetry. Bilingual. Trans. Thomas Hoeksema. Mundus Artium Press: Athens, Ohio, 1975. *Sólo esta luz*, 1969.

Poems in the Lap of Death – Poetry. Trans. Thomas Hoeksema. Latin American Literary Review Press: Pittsburgh, 1980. *Poemas en el regazo de la muerte*, 1977.

FUENTES, Carlos (Mexico 1929–)

Where the Air is Clear, a Novel – Fiction. Trans. Sam Hileman. Farrar, Straus & Giroux: New York, 1960. *La región más transparente*, 1958.

The Death of Artemio Cruz – Fiction. Trans. Sam Hileman. Farrar, Straus & Giroux: New York, 1964; Collins: London, 1964; Secker & Warburg: London, 1977; Panther: London, 1969. *La muerte de Artemio Cruz*, 1962.

Aura – Fiction. Trans. Lysander Kemp. Farrar, Straus & Giroux: New York, 1966. *Aura*, 1962.

A Change of Skin – Fiction. Trans. Sam Hileman. Cape: London, 1968; Farrar, Straus & Giroux: New York, 1968; André Deutsch: London, 1986. *Cambio de piel*, 1967.

The Good Conscience – Fiction. Trans. Sam Hileman. Farrar, Straus & Giroux: New York, 1971; André Deutsch: London, 1986. *Las buenas conciencias*, 1959.

Holy Place, in *Triple Cross* – Fiction. Trans. Suzanne Jill Levine. Dutton: New York, 1972. *Zona sagrada*, 1967.

Terra Nostra – Fiction. Trans. Margaret Sayers Peden. Farrar, Straus & Giroux: New York, 1976; Secker & Warburg: London, 1977; Penguin Books: Harmondsworth, 1978. *Terra nostra*, 1975.

The Hydra Head – Fiction. Trans. Margaret Sayers Peden. Farrar, Straus & Giroux: New York, 1978; Secker & Warburg: London, 1979. *La cabeza de la hidra*, 1978.

Burnt Water – Fiction. Trans. Margaret Sayers Peden. Farrar, Straus & Giroux: New York, 1980; Secker & Warburg: London, 1981. *Agua quemada*, 1981 and *Los días enmascarados*, 1954.

Distant Relations – Fiction. Trans. Margaret Sayers Peden. Farrar, Straus & Giroux: New York, 1982; Secker & Warburg: London, 1982; Abacus: London, 1984. *Una familia lejana*, 1980.

Latin America: At War with the Past – Essay. CBC Enterprises: Toronto, 1985.

Old Gringo – Fiction. Trans. Margaret Sayers Peden. Farrar, Straus & Giroux: New York, 1986; André Deutsch: London, 1986; Picador: London, 1987. *Gringo viejo*, 1986.

Myself with Others – Essay. Written in English. André Deutsch: London, 1988; Picador: London, 1989.

Christopher Unborn – Fiction. Trans. Alfred MacAdam. Farrar, Straus & Giroux: New York, 1989; André Deutsch: London, 1989. *Cristóbal nonato*, 1987.

G

GALEANO, Eduardo (Uruguay 1940–)

Guatemala: Occupied Country – Essay. Trans. Cedric Belfrage. Monthly Review Press: New York & London, 1969. *Guatemala, país ocupado*, 1967.

Open Veins of Latin America. 5 Centuries of the Pillage of a Continent – Essay. Trans. Cedric Belfrage. Monthly Review Press: New York & London, 1974. *Las venas abiertas de América Latina*, 1971.

Days and Nights of Love and War – Fiction. Trans. Judith Brisler. Monthly Review Press: New York, 1983; Pluto Press: London, 1983. *Días y noches de amor y de guerra*, 1978.

Genesis – Essay. Trans. Cedric Belfrage. Pantheon Books: New York, 1985; Methuen: London, 1987. *Memoria del fuego I. Los nacimientos*, 1982.

Faces and Masks – Essay. Trans. Cedric Belfrage. Quartet: London, 1987; Minerva: London, 1989. *Memoria del fuego II. Las caras y las máscaras*, 1984.

Memory of Fire: Century of the Wind – Essay. Trans. Cedric Belfrage. Pantheon Books: New York, 1988; Quartet Books: London, 1989. *Memoria del fuego III. El siglo del viento*, 1986.

GALINDO, Sergio (Mexico 1926–)

The Precipice (El bordo) – Fiction. Trans. John and Carolyn Brushwood. Univ. of Texas Press: Austin, 1969. *El bordo*, 1960.

Rice Powder (Polvos de arroz) – Fiction. Trans. Bert and Lara Patrick. Introd. John S. Brushwood. Perivale Press: Van Nuys, Calif., 1978. *Polvos de arroz*, 1958.

Mexican Masquerade (La comparsa) – Fiction. Trans. John and Carolyn

Brushwood. Latin American Literary Review Press: Pittsburgh, 1984. *La comparsa*, 1964.

GALLEGOS, Rómulo (Venezuela 1884–1968)

Doña Bárbara – Fiction. Trans. Robert Malloy. J. Cape & H. Smith: New York, 1931; F. S. Croft: New York, 1942; Peter Smith: Magnolia, Mass., 1948. *Doña Bárbara*, 1929.

Canaima – Fiction. Trans. Jaime Tello. North American Association of Venezuela: Caracas, 1984. *Canaíma*, 1935.

GALVÁN, Manuel de Jesús (Dominican Republic 1834–1910)

The Cross and the Sword – Fiction. Trans. Robert Graves. Indiana Univ. Press: Bloomington, 1954. *Enriquillo, leyenda histórica dominicana*, 1882.

GÁLVEZ, Manuel (Argentina 1882–1962)

Nacha Regules – Fiction. Trans. Leo Ongley. Dutton: New York, 1922; J. M. Dent: London, 1923. *Nacha Regules*, 1919.

Holy Wednesday – Fiction. Trans. Warre B. Wells. Appleton: New York, 1934; John Lane: London, 1934. *Miércoles santo*, 1930.

GARCÍA MÁRQUEZ, Gabriel (Colombia 1928–)

No One Writes to the Colonel, and other Stories – Fiction. Trans. J. S. Bernstein. Harper & Row: New York, 1968; Cape: London, 1971; Picador: London, 1983. *El coronel no tiene quien le escriba*, 1961.

One Hundred Years of Solitude – Fiction. Trans. Gregory Rabassa. Harper & Row: New York, 1970; Cape: London, 1970; Picador: London, 1978. *Cien años de soledad*, 1967.

Leaf Storm and Other Stories – Fiction. Trans. Gregory Rabassa. Harper & Row: New York, 1972; Picador: London, 1983. *La hojarasca*, 1955.

The Autumn of the Patriarch – Fiction. Trans. Gregory Rabassa. Harper & Row: New York, 1976; Avon Books: New York, 1977; Cape: London, 1977; Picador: London, 1983. *El otoño del patriarca*, 1975.

Innocent Eréndira and Other Stories – Fiction. Trans. Gregory Rabassa. Harper & Row: New York, 1978; Cape: London, 1979; Picador: London,

1983. *La increíble y triste historia de la Cándida Eréndira y de su abuela desalmada*, 1972.

In Evil Hour – Fiction. Trans. Gregory Rabassa. Avon Books: New York, 1980; Cape: London, 1980; Picador: London, 1983. *La mala hora*, 1962.

Chronicle of a Death Foretold – Fiction. Trans. Gregory Rabassa. Knopf: New York, 1982; Cape: London, 1982; Picador: London, 1983. *Crónica de una muerte anunciada*, 1981.

Collected Stories – Fiction. Trans. Gregory Rabassa and J S. Bernstein. Harper & Row: New York, 1984.

The Story of a Shipwrecked Sailor – Fiction. Trans. Randolph Hogan. Knopf: New York, 1986; Cape: London, 1986. *Relato de un náufrago que estuvo diez días*, 1970.

Clandestine in Chile: Adventures of Miguel Littín – Essay. Trans. Asa Zatz. H. Holt: New York, 1987; Granta Books: London, 1989. *La aventura de Miguel Littín clandestino en Chile*, 1986.

Love in the Time of Cholera – Fiction. Trans. Edith Grossman. Knopf: New York, 1988; Cape: London, 1988; Penguin Books: London, 1989. *El amor en los tiempos del cólera*, 1985.

GARCÍA PONCE, Juan (Mexico 1932–)

Encounters – Fiction. Trans. Helen Lane. Introd. Octavio Paz. Eridanos: Hygiene, Colo., 1989. *Encuentros*, 1972.

GARRO, Elena (Mexico 1920–)

Recollections of Things to Come – Fiction. Trans. Ruth L. C. Simms. Univ. of Texas Press: Austin, 1969; Sidgwick & Jackson: London, 1978. *Los recuerdos del porvenir*, 1963.

GERCHUNOFF, Alberto (Argentina 1883–1950)

The Jewish Gauchos of the Pampas – Fiction. Trans. Prudencia de Pereda. Abelard-Schuman: New York, 1955 and London, 1959. *Los gauchos judíos*, 1910.

GOLDEMBERG, Isaac (Peru 1945–)

The Fragmented Life of Don Jacobo Lerner – Fiction. Trans. Robert S. Picciotto. Persea Books: New York, 1976; Sidgwick & Jackson: London,

1978. *La vida a plazos de don Jacobo Lerner*, 1977.

Hombre de paso/ Just Passing Through – Poetry. Bilingual. Trans. David Unger, with the author. Ediciones del Norte/Point of Contact: Hanover, NH, 1981.

Play by Play – Poetry. Trans. Hardie St. Martin. Persea Books: New York, 1985.

GOMES, Paulo Emilio Salles (Brazil 1916–77)

P's Three Women – Fiction. Trans. Margaret Abigail Neves. Avon Books: New York, 1984. *Tres mulheres de tres PPPês*, 1977.

GÓMEZ, Ermilo Abreu (Mexico 1894–1971)

Canek. History and Legend of a Maya Hero – Fiction. Trans. Mario L. Dávila and Carter Wilson. Univ. of California Press: Berkeley and Los Angeles, 1979. *Canek*, 1941.

GÓMEZ-CORREA, Enrique (Chile 1915–)

Mother Darkness – Poetry. Trans. Susana Wald. Oasis Publications: Toronto, 1975.

GONZÁLEZ, José Luis (Puerto Rico 1926–)

Ballad of Another Time – Fiction. Council Oak Books: Tulsa, Okla., 1988. *Balada de otro tiempo*, 1980.

GOROSTIZA, Carlos (Argentina 1920–)

The Bridge: a Drama in Two Acts – Theatre. Trans. Louis Curlic. Samuel French: New York, 1961. *El puente*, 1946.

GOROSTIZA, José (Mexico 1901–73)

Death without End – Poetry. Bilingual. Trans. Laura Villaseñor. Univ. of Texas Press: Austin, 1969; The Ark Press: York, 1972. *Muerte sin fin*, 1939.

GUIDO, Beatriz (Argentina 1924–88)

The House of the Angel – Fiction. Trans. Joan MacLean. McGraw-Hill: New York, 1957; André Deutsch: London, 1957. *La casa del ángel*, 1954.

End of a Day – Fiction. Trans. A. D. Towers. Scribner's: New York, 1966.
El incendio y las vísperas, 1964.

GUILLÉN, Nicolás (Cuba 1902–89)

Cuba Libre: Poems – Poetry. Trans. Langston Hughes and Ben Frederick
Carruthers. Ward Ritchie Press: Los Angeles, 1948.

¡Patria o Muerte! The Great Zoo and other Poems – Poetry. Trans. & ed.
Robert Marquez. Monthly Review Press: New York, 1972.

Man-Making Words: Selected Poems of Nicolás Guillén – Poetry. Trans.,
annotated with introd. by Robert Marquez and David Arthur McMurray.
Univ. of Massachusetts Press: Amherst, 1972.

Tengo – Poetry. Trans. & ed. Richard J. Carr. Broadside Press: Detroit,
1974. *Tengo*, 1964.

The Daily Daily – Essay. Trans. Vera M. Kutzinski. Univ. of California
Press: Berkeley, 1989. *El diario que a diario*, 1972.

GÜIRALDES, Ricardo (Argentina 1886–1927)

Don Segundo Sombra: Shadows on the Pampa – Fiction. Trans. Harriet de
Onís. Farrar & Rinehart: New York, 1935; Constable: London, 1935; Penguin Books: Harmondsworth, 1948; New American Library: New York,
1966. *Don Segundo Sombra*, 1926.

GUZMÁN, Martín Luis (Mexico 1887–1977)

The Eagle and the Serpent – Fiction. Trans. Harriet de Onís. Knopf: New
York, 1930; Dolphin Books: New York, 1965. *El águila y la serpiente*,
1928.

Memoirs of Pancho Villa – Fiction. Trans. V. Taylor. Univ. of Texas Press:
Austin, 1965. *Memorias de Pancho Villa*, 1938-40.

H

HAHN, Oscar (Chile 1938–)

The Art of Dying – Poetry. Trans. James Hoggard. Latin American Literary Review Press: Pittsburgh, 1988. *Arte de morir*, 1977.

HERNÁNDEZ, José (Argentina 1834–86)

Martín Fierro. An Epic of the Argentine – Poetry. Trans. & ed. Henry Holmes. New York Hispanic Society: New York, 1923. *Martín Fierro*, 1872–79.

The Gaucho Martín Fierro – Poetry. Trans. & adapt. Walter Owen. Shakespeare Head Press: London, 1935; Gordon Press: New York, 1977.

The Gaucho Martín Fierro – Poetry. Trans. Catherine E. Ward. State Univ. of New York Press: Albany, 1967.

The Gaucho Martín Fierro – Poetry. Trans. Frank Carrino, Alberto Carlos and Norman Mangouro. State Univ. of New York: Albany, 1974.

HUIDOBRO, Vicente (Chile 1893–1948)

The Mirror of a Mage – Fiction. Trans. Warre B. Wells. Eyre & Spottiswoode: London, 1931; Houghton Mifflin: New York, 1931. *Cagliostro*, 1934

Portrait of a Paladin – Fiction. Trans. Warre B. Wells. Eyre & Spottiswoode: London, 1931; Horace Liverright: New York, 1932. *Mío Cid Campeador*, 1929.

Arctic Poems – Poetry. Trans. William Witherup. Desert Review Press: Austin, Tex., 1974. *Poemas árticos*, 1918.

The Selected Poetry of Vicente Huidobro – Poetry. Ed. David M. Guss, with an introd. Trans. W. S. Merwin, Jerome Rothenberg, Carlos Hagen,

Eliot Weinberger and others. New Directions: New York, 1981.

Altazor, or A Voyage in a Parachute, a Poem in VII Cantos – Poetry. Bilingual. Trans. Eliot Weinberger. Graywolf Press: St. Paul's, Minn., 1988. *Altazor*, 1931.

I

IBARGÜENGOITIA, Jorge (Mexico 1928–83)

The Dead Girls – Fiction. Trans. Asa Zatz. Avon Books: New York, 1983; Chatto & Windus: London, 1983. *Las muertas*, 1974.

Two Crimes – Fiction. Trans. Asa Zatz. Godine/Avon: New York, 1984; Chatto & Windus: London, 1984. *Dos crímenes*, 1979.

Lightning of August – Fiction. Trans. Irene del Corral. Chatto & Windus: London, 1986; Avon Books: New York, 1986. *Los relámpagos de agosto. Memorias de un general mexicano*, 1964.

ICAZA, Jorge (Ecuador 1906–71)

Huasipungo – Fiction. Trans. Mervyn Savill. Dennis Dobson: London, 1962. *Huasipungo*, 1934.

Huasipungo: the Villagers, a Novel – Fiction. Trans. Bernard M. Dulsey. Southern Illinois Univ. Press: Carbondale, 1964. *Huasipungo*, 1934.

ISAACS, Jorge (Colombia 1837–95)

Maria, a South American Romance – Fiction. Trans. Rollo Ogden. Introd. Thomas A. Janvier. Harper: New York, 1890. *María*, 1867.

IVO, Lêdo (Brazil 1924–)

Snake's Nest – Fiction. Trans. Kern Kraphol. Peter Owen: London, 1989. *Ninho de cobras*, 1973.

_J_

JESÚS, Teresa de – pseud. (Chile)

De repente – Poetry. Bilingual. Trans. Maria Proser, Arlene Scully, James Scully. Curbstone Press: Willimantic, Conn., 1979.

JUARROZ, Roberto (Argentina 1925–)

Vertical Poetry – Poetry. Bilingual. Trans. W. S. Merwin. Kayak Books: Santa Cruz, Calif., 1977.

Vertical Poetry – Poetry. Bilingual. Trans. W. S. Merwin. North Point Press: Berkeley, Calif., 1988. *Poesía vertical*, 1958–77.

L

LAFOURCADE, Enrique (Chile 1927–)

King Ahab's Feast – Fiction. Trans. Renate and Ray Morrison. St. Martin's Press: New York, 1963. *La fiesta del rey Acab*, 1959.

LARRETA, Enrique (Argentina 1875–1961)

The Glory of Don Ramiro. A Life in the Times of Philip II – Fiction. Trans. L. B. Walton. Dutton: New York, 1924; Dent: London, 1924. *La gloria de don Ramiro*, 1908.

LEZAMA LIMA, José (Cuba 1910–76)

Paradiso – Fiction. Trans. Gregory Rabassa. Farrar, Straus & Giroux: New York, 1974; Secker & Warburg: London, 1974; Univ. of Texas Press: Austin, 1988. *Paradiso*, 1966.

LIHN, Enrique (Chile 1929–88)

This Endless Malice; 25 poems – Poetry. Trans. Serge Echeverría and William Witherup. Lillabulero Press: New Hampshire, 1969. *La pieza oscura*, 1963 and *Poesía de paso*, 1966.

If Poetry is to be Written Right; Poems – Poetry. Trans. Dave Oliphant. Texas Portfolio Press: Texas City, 1977.

The Dark Room and Other Poems – Poetry. Bilingual. Ed. Patricio Lerzundi. Trans. Jonathan Cohen, John Felstiner, David Unger. New Directions: New York, 1978. *La pieza oscura*, 1963.

LILLO, Baldomero (Chile 1867–1923)

The Devil's Pit, and Other Stories – Fiction. Trans. Esther Dillon and Angel Flores. Organization of American States: Washington, DC, 1959.

Subterra, 1904 and *Cuadros mineros, sub sole*, 1907.

LIMA, Jorge de (Brazil 1895–1953)
Brazilian Psalm – Poetry. Trans. Willis Wager. G. Schirmer: New York, 1941.

LIMA BARRETO, Alfonso Henriques de (Brazil 1881– 1922)
The Patriot – Fiction. Trans. Robert Scott Buccleuch. Rex Collings: London, 1978. *Triste fim de Policarpo Quaresma*, 1911.
Lima Barreto. Bibliography and Translations – Fiction. Ed. & trans. Maria Luisa Nunes. G. K. Hall: Boston, 1979.

LINDO, Hugo (El Salvador 1917–)
Ways of Rain – Poetry. Trans. Elizabeth Gamble Miller. Latin American Literary Review Press: Pittsburgh, 1986. *Maneras de llover*, 1969.

LINS, Osman (Brazil 1924–78)
Avalovara – Fiction. Trans. Gregory Rabassa. Knopf: New York, 1980. *Avalovara*, 1973.

LINS de REGO, José (Brazil 1901–57)
Pureza – Fiction. Trans. Lucie Marion. Hutchinson: London, 1948. *Pureza*, 1937.
Plantation Boy – Fiction. Trans. Emmi Baum. Knopf: New York, 1966. *Menino do engenho*, 1932, *Doidinho*, 1933 and *Bangüe*, 1934.

LISPECTOR, Clarice (Brazil 1917–77)
The Apple in the Dark – Fiction. Trans. Gregory Rabassa. Knopf: New York, 1967; Virago: London, 1985. *A maçã no escuro*, 1961.
Family Ties – Fiction. Trans. Giovanni Pontiero. Univ. of Texas Press: Austin, 1972; Carcanet: Manchester, 1985. *Laços de família*, 1960.
The Foreign Legion. Stories & Chronicles – Fiction. Trans. Giovanni Pontiero. Carcanet: Manchester, 1986. *A legião estrangeira*, 1964.
The Hour of the Star – Fiction. Trans. Giovanni Pontiero. Carcanet: Manchester, 1986. *A hora da estrela*, 1977.

An Apprenticeship or the Book of Delights – Fiction. Trans. Richard Mazzara and Lorri Parris. Univ. of Texas Press: Austin, 1986. *Uma aprendizagem ou O livro dos prazeres*, 1969.

The Passion According to G. H. – Fiction. Trans. Ronald W. Souza. Univ. of Minnesota Press: Minneapolis, 1988. *A paixão segundo G. H.*, 1964.

LOBATO, José Bento Monteiro (Brazil 1882–1948)

Brazilian Short Stories – Fiction. Trans. anon. Haldeman-Julius: Girard, Kans., 1925. *Urupês*, 1918.

LÓPEZ y FUENTES, Gregorio (Mexico 1897–1966)

El indio – Fiction. Trans. Anita Brenner. Bobbs-Merrill: Indianapolis, 1937; Ungar: New York, 1961; publ. as *They That Reap*. Harrap: London, 1937. *El indio*, 1935.

LÓPEZ PORTILLO, José (Mexico 1920–)

Quetzalcoatl – Fiction. Trans. Eliot Weinberger and Diana Goodrich. Seabury Press: New York, 1976. *Quetzalcóatl*, 1965.

Don Q – Fiction. Trans. Eliot Weinberger and Wilfredo Corral. Seabury Press: New York, 1976. *Don Q*, 1965.

M

MACHADO de ASSIS, Joaquim Maria (Brazil 1839–1908)

Epitaph of a Small Winner – Fiction. Trans. William Grossman. Noonday Press: New York, 1952; W. H. Allen: London, 1953; Penguin Books: Harmondsworth, 1968; Hogarth Press: London, 1985. *Memórias póstumas de Brás Cubas*, 1881.

Dom Casmurro – Fiction. Trans. Helen Caldwell. Noonday Press: New York, 1953; W. H. Allen: London, 1953; Univ. of California Press: Berkeley, 1966. *Dom Casmurro*, 1900.

Philosopher or Dog – Fiction. Trans. Clotilde Wilson. Farrar, Straus & Giroux: New York, 1954; publ. as *The Heritage of Quincas Borba*, W. H. Allen: London, 1954. *Quincas Borba*, 1891.

The Psychiatrist and Other Stories – Fiction. Trans. William L. Grossman and Helen Caldwell. Univ of California Press: Berkeley & Los Angeles, 1963; Peter Owen: London, 1963.

Esau and Jacob – Fiction. Trans. Helen Caldwell. Univ. of California Press: Berkeley, 1965; Peter Owen: London, 1966. *Esaú e Jacó*, 1904.

The Hand and the Glove – Fiction. Trans. Albert Bagby Jr. Univ. Press of Kentucky: Lexington, 1970. *A Mão e a luva*, 1874.

Counselor Ayres's Memorial – Fiction. Trans. Helen Caldwell. Univ. of California Press: Berkeley & Los Angeles, 1972. *Memorial de Ayres*, 1908.

Yayá García – Fiction. Trans. Robert Scott Buccleuch. Peter Owen: London, 1976. *Iaiá García*, 1878.

Yayá García – Fiction. Trans. Albert Bagby Jr. University Press of Kentucky: Lexington, 1977. *Iaiá García*, 1878.

The Devil's Church and Other Stories – Fiction. Trans. Jack Schmitt and Lorie Ishmatsu. Univ. of Texas Press: Austin, 1977; Carcanet: Manchester, 1985; Grafton Books: London, 1987.

Helena – Fiction. Trans. Helen Caldwell. Univ. of California Press: Berkeley & Los Angeles, 1984. *Helena*, 1876.

MAGDALENA, Mauricio (Mexico 1906–)

Sunburst – Fiction. Trans. Anita Brenner. Viking: New York, 1944; L. Drummond: London, 1945. *El resplandor*, 1937.

MALLEA, Eduardo (Argentina 1903–82)

The Bay of Silence – Fiction. Trans. Stuart Edgar Grummon. Knopf: New York, 1944. *La bahía del silencio*, 1940.

All Green Shall Perish and other Novellas and Stories – Fiction. Trans. John Hughes, Harriet de Onís, Alis de Solá and María Mercedes Aspiazu. Knopf: New York, 1966. *Todo verdor perecerá*, 1941; *Fiesta en noviembre*, 1938 and *Chaves*, 1953.

All Green Shall Perish – Fiction. Trans. Harriet de Onís. Calder & Boyars: London, 1967. *Todo verdor perecerá*, 1941.

Fiesta in November – Fiction. Trans. Alis de Solá. Calder & Boyars: London, 1969. *Fiesta en noviembre*, 1938.

Chaves and Other Stories – Fiction. Trans. María Mercedes Aspiazu. Calder & Boyars: London, 1970. *Chaves*, 1953.

History of an Argentine Passion – Essay. Trans. Myron I. Lichtblau. Latin American Literary Review Press: Pittsburgh, 1983. *Historia de una pasión argentina*, 1937.

MÁRMOL, José (Argentina 1818–71)

Amalia: a Romance of the Argentine – Fiction. Trans. Mary J. Serrano. Dutton: New York, 1919; Gordon Press: New York, 1977. *Amalia*, 1851-55.

MARQUÉS, René (Puerto Rico 1919–79)

The Oxcart – Theatre. Trans. Charles Pilditch. Scribner's: New York, 1969. *La carreta*, 1952.

The Docile Puerto Rican – Essay. Trans. & introd. Barbara Bockus Aponte. Temple Univ. Press: Philadelphia, 1976. Title and date of original unknown.

MARTÍ, José (Cuba 1853–95)

The America of José Martí: Selected Writings of José Martí – Essay. Trans. & ed. Juan de Onís. Noonday Press: New York, 1953; Funk & Wagnalls: New York, 1968.

Inside the Monster: Writings on the United States and American Imperialism – Essay. Ed. & introd. Philip Foner. Trans. Elinor Randall, Luis Baraly, Juan de Onís and Roslyn Foner. Monthly Review Press: New York, 1975.

Our America: Writings on Latin America and the Struggle for Cuban Independence – Essay. Ed. & introd. Philip Foner. Trans. Elinor Randall, Juan de Onís and Roslyn Held Forner. Monthly Review Press: New York, 1977.

Major Poems. A Bilingual Edition – Poetry. Ed. with introd. Philip Foner. Trans. Elinor Randall. Holmes & Meier: New York, 1982.

MARTÍNEZ ESTRADA, Ezequiel (Argentina 1895–1964)

X-Ray of the Pampa – Essay. Trans. Alain Swietlicki. Introd. Thomas F. McGann. Univ. of Texas Press: Austin, 1972. *Radiografía de la pampa*, 1933.

Holy Saturday and Other Stories – Fiction. Trans. Leland H. Chambers. Introd. Peter G. Earle. Latin American Literary Review Press: Pittsburgh, 1988. *Sábado de gloria*, 1956 and *Cuatro novelas*, 1968.

MARTÍNEZ MORENO, Carlos (Uruguay 1917–86)

El infierno – Fiction. Trans. Ann Wright. Introd. John King. Readers International: London, 1988. *El color que el infierno me escondiera*, 1981.

MARTÍNEZ, Tomás Eloy (Argentina 1934–)

The Perón Novel – Fiction. Trans. Asa Zatz. Pantheon Books: New York, 1988. *La novela de Perón*, 1985.

MASSO, Gerardo di (Argentina 1949–)

The Shadow by the Door – Fiction. Trans. Richard Jacques. Zed Books: London, 1985; Curbstone Press: Willimantic, Conn., 1986. *La penumbra*, 1983.

MASTRETA, Angeles (Mexico 1949–)

Mexican Bolero – Fiction. Trans. Ann Wright. Viking: London, 1989. *Arráncame la vida*, 1985.

MATOS PAOLI, Francisco (Puerto Rico 1915–)

Songs of Madness and Other Poems – Poetry. Bilingual. Trans. Frances Aparicio. Latin American Literary Review Press: Pittsburgh, 1985. *Cantos de la locura*, 1962.

MATTO de TURNER, Clorinda (Peru 1854–1909)

Birds without a Nest. A Story of Indian Life and Priestly Oppression in Peru – Fiction. Trans. J. G. Hudson. Charles J. Thynn: London, 1904; Schneider: New York, 1968. *Aves sin nido*, 1889.

MEDINA, Enrique (Argentina 1942–)

The Duke: Memories and Anti-Memories of a Participant in the Repression – Fiction. Trans. David William Foster. Zed Books: London, 1985. *El duque*, 1976.

MEIRELES, Cecília (Brazil 1901–64)

Poemas em tradução/Poems in Translation – Poetry. Bilingual. Trans., ed. & introd. Henry Keith and Raymond Sayers. Brazilian-American Cultural Institute: Washington, DC, 1977.

MISTRAL, Gabriela – pseud. for Lucila Godoy Alcayaga (Chile 1889–1957)

Selected Poems of Gabriela Mistral – Poetry. Trans. Langston Hughes. Indiana Univ. Press: Bloomington, 1957.

Selected Poems of Gabriela Mistral – Poetry. Bilingual. Trans. & ed. Doris Dana. Johns Hopkins Univ. Press: Baltimore, Md., 1971.

MONTANER, Carlos Alberto (Cuba 1943–)

The Witches' Poker and Other Stories – Fiction. Trans. Bob Robinson. Inter-American Univ. Press: Hato Rey, Puerto Rico, 1973. *Póker de brujas, 1968* and *Instantáneas al borde del abismo*, 1970.

Secret Report on the Cuban Revolution – Essay. Trans. E. Zayas-Bazán. Transaction: New Brunswick, NJ, 1980. *Informe secreto sobre la revolución cubana*, 1970

Two Hundred Years of Gringos. Trans. Gastón Fernández de la Torriente. Univ. Press of America: Lanham, Md., 1983. *200 años de gringos*, 1976.

MONTELLO, Josué (Brazil 1917–54)

Coronation Quay – Fiction. Trans. Myriam Henderson. Rex Collings: London, 1975. *Cais da sagração*, 1971.

MONTERROSO, Augusto (Guatemala 1922–)

The Black Sheep and Other Fables – Fiction. Trans. I. Bradbury. Doubleday: Garden City, NY, 1971. *La oveja negra y demás fábulas*, 1969.

MONTES de OCA, Marco Antonio (Mexico 1932–)

On the Ruins of Babylon with Tiresias – Poetry. Trans. Rolf Henneques. Wattle Grove Press: Tasmania, 1964.

The Heart of the Flute – Poetry. Bilingual. Trans. Laura Villaseñor. Introd. Octavio Paz. Ohio Univ. Press: Athens, Ohio, 1978. *Pedir el fuego*, 1968.

Twenty-one Poems – Poetry. Trans. Laura Villaseñor. Latin American Literary Review Press: Pittsburgh, 1982.

MOREJÓN, Nancy (Cuba 1944–)

Where the Island Sleeps like a Wing – Poetry. Trans. Kathleen Weaver. Black Scholar Press: San Francisco, 1985.

MORO, César – pseud. for César Quispes Asiú (Peru 1904–56)

Amour à Mort (Love till Death) – Poetry. Trans. Frances Lefevre. TVRT Press: New York, 1973. *Amour à Mort*, 1957.

The Scandalous Life of César Moro – Poetry. Trans. Philip Ward. Oleander Press: Cambridge, 1976. *La tortuga ecuestre*, 1957.

MOYANO, Daniel (Argentina 1930–)

The Devil's Trill – Fiction. Trans. Giovanni Pontiero. Serpent's Tail: London, 1988. *El trino del diablo*, 1974

MÚJICA LÁINEZ, Manuel (Argentina 1910–84)

Bomarzo, a Novel – Fiction. Trans. Gregory Rabassa. Simon & Schuster: New York, 1969; Weidenfeld & Nicolson: London, 1970. *Bomarzo*, 1962.

The Wandering Unicorn – Fiction. Trans. Mary Fitton. Lester & Orpen Dennys: Toronto, 1982; Chatto & Windus: London, 1983. *El unicornio*, 1965.

MUÑIZ-HUBERMAN, Angelina (Spain/Mexico 1936–)

Enclosed Garden. Short Stories by Angelina Muñiz – Fiction. Trans. Lois Parkinson Zamora. Latin American Literary Review Press: Pittsburgh, 1988. *Huerto cerrado, huerto sellado*, 1985.

MURENA, Hector (Argentina 1923–75)

The Laws of the Night – Fiction. Trans. Rachel Coffyn. Charles Scribner's: New York, 1970. *Las leyes de la noche*, 1958.

N

NERUDA, Pablo – pseud. for Neftalí Ricardo Reyes (Chile 1904–73)

Residence on Earth and Other Poems – Poetry. Bilingual. Trans. Angel Flores. New Directions: Norfolk, Conn., 1946; Gordian Press: New York, 1976. *Residencia en la tierra*, 1935.

Let the Rail-Splitter Awake and Other Poems – Poetry. Trans. J. M. Bernstein. Masses & Mainstream: New York, 1951; Journeyman: London, 1988. *Canto general*, 1950.

The Elemental Odes. A Selection – Poetry. Bilingual. Trans. Carlos Lozano. Las Américas: New York, 1961. *Odas elementales*, 1954.

Residence on Earth – Poetry. Trans. Clayton Eshelman. Amber House Press: San Francisco, 1962. *Residencia en la tierra*, 1935.

Bestiary/bestiario – Poetry. Bilingual. Trans. Elsa Neuberger. Harcourt Brace Jovanovich: New York, 1965. *Bestiario*, 1958.

We are Many – Poetry. Bilingual. Trans. Alastair Reid. Cape Goliard: London, 1967; Grossman: New York, 1968.

The Heights of Macchu Picchu – Poetry. Bilingual. Trans. Nathaniel Tarn. Preface Robert Pring-Mill. Farrar, Straus & Giroux: New York, 1967; Cape: London, 1966. *Alturas de Macchu Picchu*, 1945.

Pablo Neruda - Twenty Poems – Poetry. Bilingual. Trans. Robert Bly and Charles Wright. Sixties Press: Maddison, Minn., 1967; Rapp & Whiting: London, 1968.

Twenty Love Poems and a Song of Despair – Poetry. Trans. W. S. Merwin. Cape: London, 1969; Grossman: New York, 1971; Penguin Books: Harmondsworth, 1976. *Veinte poemas de amor y una canción desesperada*, 1924.

The Early Poems – Poetry. Trans. David Ossman and Carlos Hagen. New Rivers Press: New York, 1969.

Selected Poems – Poetry. Bilingual. Trans. & ed. Ben Belitt. Grove Press: New York, 1969.

Pablo Neruda: a New Decade. Poems 1958–1967 – Poetry. Bilingual. Trans. & ed. Ben Belitt and Alastair Reid. Grove Press: New York, 1970.

Selected Poems – Poetry. Bilingual. Ed. Nathaniel Tarn. Trans. Anthony Kerrigan, W. S. Merwin, Alastair Reid, Nathaniel Tarn. Cape: London, 1970; Delacorte Press: New York, 1972; Penguin Books: Harmondsworth, 1975.

Neruda and Vallejo: Selected Poems – Poetry. Bilingual. Ed. Robert Bly. Trans. Robert Bly, John Knoepfle and James Wright. Ed. Robert Bly. Beacon Press: Boston, 1971.

The Captain's Verses – Poetry. Bilingual. Trans. Donald Walsh. New Directions: New York, 1972. *Los versos del capitán*, 1953.

The Splendour and Death of Joaquín Murieta – Theatre. Trans. Ben Belitt. Farrar, Straus & Giroux: New York, 1972; Alcove Press: London, 1973. *Fulgor y muerte de Joaquín Murieta*, 1967.

Extravagaria – Poetry. Trans. Alastair Reid. Cape: London, 1972; Farrar, Straus & Giroux: New York, 1974. *Estravagario*, 1958.

Residence on Earth – Poetry. Trans. Donald Walsh. New Directions: New York, 1973; Souvenir Press: London, 1976. *Residencia en la tierra*, 1935.

Five decades. A Selection. Poems 1925–1970 – Poetry. Trans. Ben Belitt. Grove Press: New York, 1974.

Fully Empowered – Poetry. Bilingual. Trans. Alastair Reid. Farrar, Straus & Giroux: New York, 1975. *Plenos poderes*, 1962.

Song of Protest – Poetry. Trans. & introd. Miguel Algarín. William Morrow: New York, 1976. *Canción de gesta*, 1960.

Memoirs – Essay. Trans. Hardie St. Martin. Farrar, Straus & Giroux: New York, 1976; Souvenir Press: London, 1977; Penguin Books: Harmondsworth, 1989. *Confieso que he vivido. Memorias*, 1974.

Incitement to Nixoncide – Poetry. Trans. Steve Kowit. Quixote Press: Houston, 1977. *Incitación al Nixoncidio y alabanza de la revolución chilena*, 1973.

The Heights of Macchu Picchu – Poetry. Bilingual. Trans. John Felstiner. In *Translating Neruda. The Way to Macchu Picchu*. Stanford Univ. Press: Palo Alto, Calif., 1980.

Isla Negra: a Notebook – Poetry. Bilingual. Trans. Alastair Reid. Farrar, Straus & Giroux: New York, 1981; Souvenir Press: London, 1982. *Memorial de Isla Negra*, 1964.

Selections: Poems from Canto General – Poetry. Trans. J. C. R. Greene. Aquila Publishing Co.: Isle of Skye, 1982. *Canto general*, 1950.

Passions and Impressions – Essay. Eds. Matilde Neruda and Miguel Otero Silva. Trans. Margaret Sayers Peden. Farrar, Straus & Giroux: New York, 1983. *Para nacer he nacido*, 1978.

Still Another Day – Poetry. Trans. William O'Daly. Copper Canyon Press: Port Townsend, Wash., 1984. *Aún*, 1969.

Eight Odes – Poetry. Trans. Ken Norris. Muses' Company: St Anne de Bellevue, 1984.

Art of Birds – Poetry. Trans. Jack Schmitt. Univ. of Texas Press: Austin, 1985. *Arte de pájaros*, 1966.

The Separate Rose – Poetry. Trans. William O'Daley. Copper Canyon Press: Port Townsend, Wash., 1985. *La rosa separada*, 1973.

One Hundred Love Sonnets / Cien sonetos de amor – Poetry. Bilingual. Trans. Stephen Tapscott. Univ. of Texas Press: Austin, 1986. *Cien sonetos de amor*, 1960.

Winter Day – Poetry. Trans. William O'Daley. Copper Canyon Press: Port Townsend, Wash., 1986. *Jardín de invierno*, 1974.

Stones of Chile – Poetry. Trans. Dennis Maloney. White Pine Press: New York, 1986. *Las piedras de Chile*, 1961.

Stones of the Skies – Poetry. Trans. James Nolar. Copper Canyon Press: Port Townsend, Wash., 1987. *Las piedras del cielo*, 1970.

The Sea and the Bells – Poetry. Trans. William O'Daley. Copper Canyon Press: Port Townsend, Wash., 1988. *El mar y las campanas*, 1973.

NERVO, Amado (Mexico 1870–1919)

Plenitude – Poetry. Bilingual. Trans. William Rice. J. R. Miller: Los Angeles, 1928. *Plenitud*, 1918.

Confessions of a Modern Poet – Poetry. Trans. Dorothy Kress. Bruce Humphries: Boston, 1935.

NOVO, Salvador (Mexico 1904–74)

Nuevo amor – Poetry. Trans. Edna Worthley Underwood. Mosher Press: Portland, Ore., 1935. *Nuevo amor*, 1933.

NÚÑEZ, Raúl (Argentina 1946–)

The Lonely Hearts Club – Fiction. Trans. Ed Emery. Serpent's Tail: London, 1989. *Sinatra*, 1984.

O

OCAMPO, Silvina (Argentina 1903–)

Leopoldina's Dream – Fiction. Trans. Daniel Balderston. Penguin Books: Toronto, 1988. *Autobiografía de Irene*, 1948; *La furia*, 1959; *Las invitadas*, 1961 and *Los días de la noche*, 1970.

OLINTO, Antônio (Brazil 1919–)

The Water House – Fiction. Trans. Dorothy Heapy. Rex Collings: London, 1970; Nelson & Sons: London, 1982. *A casa da água*, 1969.

Theories and Other Poems – Poetry. Bilingual. Trans. Jean McQuiller. Rex Collings: London, 1972. *Teorias*, 1967.

The Day of Wrath – Poetry. Trans. Richard Chappell. Rex Collings: London, 1986. *O dia da ira*, 1958.

The King of Ketu – Fiction. Trans. Richard Chappell. Rex Collings: London, 1987. *O rei de Keto*, 1980.

ONETTI, Juan Carlos (Uruguay 1909–)

The Shipyard – Fiction. Trans. Rachel Caffyn. Scribner's: New York, 1968. *El astillero*, 1961.

A Brief Life – Fiction. Trans. Hortense Carpentier. Grossman: New York, 1976. *La vida breve*, 1950.

OQUENDO de AMAT, Carlos (Peru 1905–36)

Five Metres of Poems – Poetry. Trans. David Guss. Turkey Press: Isla Vista, Calif., 1986. *Cinco metros de poemas*, 1927.

ORPHÉE, Elvira (Argentina 1930–)

El Angel's Last Conquest – Fiction. Trans. Magda Bogin. Ballantine: New York, 1985. *La última conquista de El Angel*, 1977.

ORTEGA, Julio (Peru 1942–)

The Land in the Day – Essay/Poetry. Trans. author and Ewing Cambell. New Latin Quarter Editions: Austin, Tex., 1978. *Tierra en el día*, 1975.

Poetics of Change – Essay. Trans. Galen D. Greaser. Univ. of Texas Press: Austin, 1984.

P

PACHECO, José Emilio (Mexico 1939–)

Tree between Two Walls – Poetry. Trans. Gordon Brotherston and Ed Dorn. Black Sparrow Press: Santa Barbara, Calif., 1969.

Don't Ask Me How the Time Goes By. Poems 1964–1968 – Poetry. Bilingual. Trans. Alastair Reid. Columbia Univ. Press: New York, 1978. *No me preguntes cómo pasa el tiempo*, 1969.

Signals from the Flames – Poetry. Trans. Thomas Hoeksema. Latin American Review Literary Press: Pittsburgh, 1980.

Battles in the Desert and Other Stories – Fiction. Trans. Katherine Silver. New Directions: New York, 1987. *Las batallas en el desierto*, 1981.

Selected Poems – Poetry. Ed. George McWhirter. Trans. George McWhirter, Thomas Hoeksema, Alastair Reid, Linda Scheer, Ed Dorn, Gordon Brotherston, Katherine Silver, Elizabeth Umlas. New Directions: New York, 1987.

PADILLA, Heberto (Cuba 1932–)

Sent off the Field. A Selection from the Poetry of Heberto Padilla – Poetry. Trans. J. M. Cohen. André Deutsch: London, 1971.

Poetry and Politics: Selected Poems of Heberto Padilla – Poetry. Trans. Frank Calzon, Laura Ymaxo, María Luisa Alvarez. Georgetown Univ. Cuban Series: Washington, DC, 1977.

Legacies: Selected Poems – Poetry. Bilingual. Trans. Alastair Reid and Andrew Hurley. Farrar, Straus & Giroux: New York, 1982; Faber & Faber: London, 1982.

Heroes are Grazing in my Garden – Fiction. Trans. Andrew Hurley. Farrar, Straus & Giroux: New York, 1984. *En mi jardín pastan los héroes*, 1981.

PADILLA, Telmo (Brazil 1930–)

Bird / Night – Poetry. Bilingual. Trans. Fernando Camacho. Rex Collings: London, 1976. *Onde tombam as pássaros*, 1974.

PALMA, Ricardo (Peru 1833–1919)

The Knights of the Cape and 37 Other Selections from the Tradiciones peruanas – Fiction. Trans. Harriet de Onís. Knopf: New York, 1945. *Las tradiciones peruanas*, 1872-1910.

PARRA, Nicanor (Chile 1914–)

Anti-poems – Poetry. Trans. Jorge Eliott. City Lights Books: San Francisco, 1960. *Poemas y antipoemas*, 1954.

Poems and Antipoems – Poetry. Bilingual. Ed. Miller Williams. Trans. Lawrence Ferlinghetti, Allen Ginsberg, Thomas Merton, Denise Levertov, W. S. Merwin, William Carlos Williams and editor. New Directions: New York, 1967; Cape: London, 1967. *Poemas y antipoemas*, 1954.

Emergency Poems – Poetry. Bilingual. Trans. & ed. Miller Williams. New Directions: New York, 1972; Marion Boyars: London, 1977. *Poemas de emergencia*, 1972.

Sermons and Homilies of the Christ of Elqui – Poetry. Bilingual. Trans. Sandra Reyes. Univ. of Missouri Press: Columbia, 1984. *Sermones y prédicas del Cristo de Elqui*, 1979.

Antipoems: New and Selected – Poetry. Ed. David Unger. Trans. Lawrence Ferlinghetti, Allen Ginsberg, Thomas Merton, W. S. Merwin, Hardie St. Martin, David Unger, William Carlos Williams, Miller Williams and others. Introd. Frank MacShane. New Directions: New York, 1985.

PARRA, Teresa de la (Venezuela 1889–1936)

Mama Blanca's Souvenirs – Fiction. Trans. Harriet de Onís. Pan American Union: Washington, DC, 1959. *Las memorias de Mamá Blanca*, 1928.

PARTNOY, Alicia (Argentina 1955–)

The Little School. Tales of Disappearance and Survival in Argentina – Fiction/Essay. Trans. by author, with Lois Athey and Sandra Braunstein. Cleis Press: Pittsburgh, 1986; Virago: London, 1988.

PAZ, Octavio (Mexico 1914–)

The Labyrinth of Solitude: Life and Thought in Mexico – Essay. Trans. Lysander Kemp. Grove Press: New York, 1961; Allen Lane: Harmondsworth, 1967; Penguin Books: London, 1985. *El laberinto de la soledad*, 1950.

Sun Stone – Poetry. Trans. Muriel Rukeyser. New Directions: New York, 1962. *Piedra de sol*, 1957

Sun-Stone – Poetry. Trans. Peter Miller. Contact Press: Toronto, 1963.

Selected Poems – Poetry. Bilingual. Trans. Muriel Rukeyser, Lysander Kemp, Denise Levertov, Paul Blackburn. Indiana Univ. Press: Bloomington, 1963.

Piedra de sol. The Sun Stone – Poetry. Bilingual. Trans. Donald Gardner. Cosmos Publications: York, 1969. *Piedra de sol*, 1957.

Marcel Duchamp: or The Castle of Purity – Essay. Trans. Donald Gardner. Cape Goliard Press: London, 1970. *Marcel Duchamp o el castillo de la pureza*, 1968.

Claude Lévi-Strauss: an Introduction – Essay. Trans. J. S. Bernstein and M. Bernstein. Cornell Univ. Press: Ithaca, NY, 1970; Cape: London, 1971. *Claude Lévi-Strauss o el nuevo festín de Esopo*, 1967.

¿Aguila o sol? Eagle or Sun? – Poetry. Trans. Eliot Weinberger. October House: New York, 1970; New Directions: New York, 1976. *¿Aguila o sol?* 1951.

Configurations – Poetry. Trans. Muriel Rukeyser, Denise Levertov, Charles Tomlinson and others. New Directions: New York, 1971; Cape: London, 1971.

Renga. A Chain of Poems by Octavio Paz, Jacques Roubaud, Edoardo Sanguineti, Charles Tomlinson – Poetry. Trans. Charles Tomlinson. George Braziller: New York, 1972; Penguin Books: Harmondsworth, 1979. *Renga*, 1972.

The Other Mexico: Critique of the Pyramid – Essay. Trans. Lysander Kemp. Grove Press: New York, 1972. *Posdata*, 1970.

Early Poems. 1935-1955 – Poetry. Trans. Muriel Rukeyser, Paul Blackburn, Lysander Kemp, Denise Levertov, William Carlos Williams. New Directions: New York, 1973.

Alternating Current – Essay. Trans. Helen Lane. Viking Press: New York, 1973; Calder & Boyars: London, 1974; Wildwood House: London, 1974. *Corriente alterna*, 1967.

The Bow and the Lyre – Essay. Trans. Ruth L. Simms. Univ of Texas Press: Austin, 1973. *El arco y la lira*, 1956.

Children of the Mire: Poetry from Romanticism to the Avant-Garde – Essay. Trans. Rachel Phillips. Harvard Univ. Press: Cambridge Mass., 1974. *Los hijos del limo: del romanticismo a la vanguardia*, 1974.

Conjunctions and Disjunctions – Essay. Trans. Helen Lane. Viking Press: New York, 1974; Calder & Boyars: London, 1974; Seaver Books: New York, 1982. *Conjunciones y disyunciones*, 1969.

Blanco – Poetry. Trans. Eliot Weinberger. Introd. Roger Shattuck. The Press: New York, 1974. *Blanco*, 1967.

The Siren and the Seashell and Other Essays on Poets and Poetry – Essay. Trans. Lysander Kemp and Margaret Sayers Peden. Univ. of Texas Press: Austin, 1976.

A Draft of Shadows and Other Poems – Poetry. Trans. Eliot Weinberger, Elizabeth Bishop, Mark Strand. New Directions: New York, 1979.

Selected Poems – Poetry. Bilingual. Ed. Charles Tomlinson. Trans. Charles Tomlinson, Elizabeth Bishop, Eliot Weinberger and others. Penguin Books: Harmondsworth, 1979.

Marcel Duchamp: Appearances Stripped Bare – Essay. Trans. Rachel Phillips and Donald Gardner. Viking: New York, 1979. *Apariencia desnuda; la obra de Marcel Duchamp*, 1973.

The Monkey Grammarian – Poetry. Trans. Helen Lane. Seaver Books: New York, 1981; Peter Owen: London, 1989. *El mono gramático*, 1974.

Airborn. Hijos del aire – Poetry. Trans. Charles Tomlinson. Anvil Press: London, 1981.

Selected Poems – Poetry. Ed. Eliot Weinberger. Trans. Eliot Weinberger, Elizabeth Bishop, Lysander Kemp and others. New Directions: New York, 1984.

One Earth, Four or Five Worlds: Reflections on Contemporary History – Essay. Trans. Helen Lane. Harcourt Brace Jovanovich: New York, 1985; Carcanet: Manchester, 1986. *Tiempo nublado*, 1983.

The Collected Poems of Octavio Paz, 1957–1987 – Poetry. Bilingual. Ed. Eliot Weinberger. Trans. Eliot Weinberger, Charles Tomlinson, Elizabeth Bishop and others. New Directions: New York, 1987; Carcanet: Manchester, 1988.

On Poets and Others – Essay. Trans. Michael Schmidt. Carcanet: Manchester, 1987.

Convergences: Essays on Art and Literature – Essay. Trans. Helen Lane. Harcourt, Brace, Jovanovich: New York, 1987; Bloomsbury: London, 1987.

A Tree Within – Poetry. Trans. Eliot Weinberger. New Directions: New York, 1988. *Arbol adentro*, 1987.

Sor Juana: or, the Traps of Faith – Essay. Trans. Margaret Sayers Peden. Harvard Univ. Press: Cambridge, Mass., 1988; publ. as *Sor Juana: Her Life and Her World*, Faber & Faber: London, 1988. *Sor Juana o las trampas de la fe*, 1986.

PENNA, Cornelio (Brazil 1896–1968)

Threshold – Fiction. Trans. Tona and Edward A. Riggio. Franklin Publishing Co: Philadelphia, 1975. *Fronteira*, 1935.

PEREIRA, Antônio Olavo (Brazil 1913–)

Marcoré – Fiction. Trans. Alfred Hower and John Saunders. Univ. of Texas Press: Austin, 1970. *Marcoré*, 1957.

PETIT MARFÁN, Magdalena (Chile 1903–68)

La Quintrala – Fiction. Trans. Lulú Vargas Vila. Macmillan: New York, 1942. *La Quintrala*, 1930.

PEYROU, Manuel (Argentina 1902–74)

Thunder of the Roses – Fiction. Trans. Donald Yates. Introd. Jorge Luis Borges. Herder & Herder: New York, 1972. *El estruendo de las rosas*, 1948.

PIÑERA, Virgilio (Cuba 1912–79)

Cold Tales – Fiction. Trans. Mark Schafer. Introd. Guillermo Cabrera Infante. Eridanos Press: Hygiene, Colo., 1988. *Cuentos fríos*, 1956.

René's Flesh – Fiction. Trans. Mark Schafer, Eridanos Press: Hygiene, Colo., 1989. *La carne de René*, 1952.

PIÑON, Nélida (Brazil 1936–)

The Republic of Dreams – Fiction. Trans. Helen Lane. Knopf: New York, 1989. *A república dos sonhos*, 1984.

PIWONKA, María Elvira (Chile 1915–)

Selected Poems – Poetry. Trans. Edward Newman Horn. Osmar Press: New York, 1967.

PIZARNIK, Alejandra (Argentina 1936–72)

A Profile – Poetry. Ed. & introd. Frank Graziano. Trans. Frank Graziano and Maria Rosa Fort. Logbridge-Rhodes: Durango, Colo., 1987.

PIZARRO, Agueda (Colombia 1941–)

Sombraventadora/Shadowinnower – Poetry. Bilingual. Trans. Barbara Stoler Miller, with the poet. Columbia Univ. Press: New York, 1979.

PONCE, Manuel (Mexico – dates unknown)

Algunos de mis poemas/Some of my Poems – Poetry. Bilingual. Trans. & introd. María Luisa Rodríguez Lee. Latin American Literary Review Press: Pittsburgh, 1987.

PONIATOWSKA, Elena (Mexico 1932–)

Massacre in Mexico – Essay. Trans. Helen Lane. Prol. Octavio Paz. Viking Press: New York, 1975. *La noche de Tlatelolco*, 1971.

Dear Diego – Fiction. Trans. Katherine Silver. Pantheon Books: New York, 1986. *Querido Diego, te abraza Quiniela y otros cuentos*, 1978.

Until We Meet Again – Fiction. Pantheon Books: New York, 1987. *Hasta no verte, Jesús mío*, 1969.

PORCHIA, Antonio (Argentina 1886-1969)

Voices – Poetry. Trans. W. S. Merwin. Follett: Chicago, 1969. *Voces*, 1943.

POSSE, Abel (Argentina 1936–)

The Dogs of Paradise – Fiction. Trans. Margaret Sayers Peden. Atheneum: New York, 1989. *Los perros del paraíso*, 1987.

PRADA, Renato (Bolivia 1937–)

The Breach – Fiction. Trans. Walter Redmond. Doubleday: Garden City, NJ, 1971. *Los fundadores del alba*, 1969.

PRADO, Pedro (Chile 1886-1952)

Country Judge; a Novel of Chile – Fiction. Trans. Lesley Bird Simpson. Univ. of California Press: Berkeley, 1968. *Un juez rural*, 1924.

PRIETO, Jenaro (Chile 1889–1946)

The Partner – Fiction. Blanca de Roig and Guy Dowler. Butterworth: London, 1931. *El socio*, 1928.

PUIG, Manuel (Argentina 1934–)

Betrayed by Rita Hayworth – Fiction. Trans. Suzanne Jill Levine. Dutton: New York, 1971; Arena: London, 1984. *La traición de Rita Hayworth*, 1968.

Heartbreak Tango; a Serial – Fiction. Trans. Suzanne Jill Levine. Dutton: New York, 1973; Arena: London, 1987. *Boquitas pintadas*, 1969.

The Buenos Aires Affair: a Detective Novel – Fiction. Trans. Suzanne Jill Levine. Dutton: New York, 1976; Faber & Faber: London, 1989. *The Buenos Aires Affair*, 1973.

Kiss of the Spider Woman – Fiction. Trans. Thomas Colchie. Knopf: New York, 1979; Arena: London, 1984. *El beso de la mujer araña*, 1976.

Eternal Curse on the Reader of These Pages – Fiction. Written in English. Random House: New York, 1982; Arena: London, 1985. *Maldición eterna a quien lea estas páginas*, 1980.

Blood of Requited Love – Fiction. Trans. Jan Grayson. Aventura: New York, 1984; Faber & Faber: London, 1989. *Sangre de amor correspondido*, 1984.

Under a Mantle of Stars – Theatre. Trans. Ronald Christ. Lumen: New York, 1983. *Bajo un manto de estrellas*, 1983.

Pubis angelical – Fiction. Trans. Elena Brunet. Random House: New York, 1986; Faber & Faber: London, 1987. *Pubis angelical*, 1979.

Kiss of the Spider Woman – Theatre. Trans. Allan Baker. Amber Lane Press: Oxford, 1987. *El beso de la mujer araña*, 1983.

Mystery of the Rose Bouquet – Theatre. Trans. Allan Baker. Faber & Faber: London, 1988. *Misterio del ramo de rosas*, 1988.

Q

QUEIROZ, Rachel de (Brazil 1910–)

The Three Marias – Fiction. Trans. Fred P. Ellison. Univ. of Texas Press: Austin, 1963. *As tres Marias*, 1939.

Dôra, Doralina – Fiction. Trans. Dorothy Scott Loos. Avon Books: New York, 1984. *Dôra, Doralina*, 1975.

QUIROGA, Horacio (Uruguay 1878–1937)

South American Jungle Tales – Fiction. Trans. Arthur Livingston. Duffield: New York, 1922; Methuen: London, 1923. *Cuentos de la selva*, 1918.

The Decapitated Chicken and Other Stories – Fiction. Trans. Margaret Sayers Peden. Univ. of Texas Press: Austin, 1976. *Cuentos de amor, de locura y de muerte*, 1917.

The Exiles and Other Stories – Fiction. Trans. & ed. J. David Danielson. Univ. of Texas Press: Austin, 1987. *Los desterrados*, 1926.

R

RAMÍREZ, Sergio (Nicaragua 1942–)

To Bury our Fathers – Fiction. Trans. Nick Caistor. Readers International: London, 1984. *¿Te dio miedo la sangre?* 1977.

Stories – Fiction. Trans. Nick Caistor. Readers International: London, 1986. *Charles Atlas también muere*, 1976.

RAMOS, Graciliano (Brazil 1892–1953)

Anguish – Fiction. Trans. L. C. Kaplin. Knopf: New York, 1946; Greenwood Press: New York, 1972. *Angústia*, 1936.

Barren Lives – Fiction. Trans. Ralph E. Dimmick. Univ. of Texas Press: Austin, 1961. *Vidas sêcas*, 1938.

Jail Prison Memoirs – Essay. Trans. Thomas Colchie. Evans: New York, 1974. *Memórias do cárcere*, 1953.

São Bernardo – Fiction. Trans. Robert Scott-Buccleuch. Peter Owen: London, 1975. *São Bernardo*, 1934.

Childhood – Fiction. Trans. Celso de Oliveira. Peter Owen: London, 1979. *Infância*, 1945.

RESENDE, Otto Laura (Brazil 1922–)

The Inspector of Orphans – Fiction. Trans. Anne Cravinho. André Deutsch: London, 1968. *O braço direito*, 1963.

REVUELTAS, José (Mexico 1914–76)

The Stone Knife – Fiction. Trans. H. R. Hays. Reynal-Hitchcock: New York, 1947. *El luto humano*, 1943.

Human Mourning – Fiction. Trans. Roberto Crespi. Foreword Octavio Paz. Univ. of Minnesota Press: Minneapolis, 1989. *El luto humano*, 1943.

REY, Marcos (Brazil 1925–)

Memoirs of a Gigolo – Fiction. Trans. Clifford E. Landers. Avon Books: New York, 1987. *Memórias de un gigolô*, 1968.

REY ROSA, Rodrigo (Guatemala 1958–)

The Beggar's Knife – Fiction. Trans. Paul Bowles. City Lights: San Francisco, 1985; Peter Owen: London, 1988. *El cuchillo del mendigo*, 1986.

Dust on her Tongue – Fiction. Trans. Paul Bowles. Peter Owen: London, 1989.

REYLES, Carlos (Uruguay 1868–1938)

Castanets – Fiction. Trans. Jacquest Le Clercq. Longmans Green: New York & London, 1929; Jacobsen: New York, 1929. *El embrujo de Sevilla*, 1922.

RIBEIRO, Darcy (Brazil 1922–)

Maíra – Fiction. Trans. E. H. Goodland and Thomas Colchie. Random House: New York, 1984; Picador: London, 1984. *Maíra*, 1978.

The Americas and Civilization – Essay. Trans. Linton and Marie McBarrett. Dutton: New York, 1971. *As Américas e a civiliação*, 1970.

RIBEIRO, João Ubaldo (Brazil 1940–)

Sergeant Getúlio – Fiction. Trans. by author. Houghton Mifflin: Boston, 1978; Faber & Faber: London, 1986. *Sargento Getúlio*, 1971.

An Invincible Memory – Fiction. Trans. by author. Harper & Row: New York, 1989; Faber & Faber: London, 1989. *O povo brasileiro*, 1984.

RIBEIRO, Stella Carr (Brazil 1932–)

Sambaqui: a Novel of Pre-History – Fiction. Trans. Claudia Van de Heuvel. Avon Books: New York, 1987. *O homem do Sambaqui*, 1975.

RIVABELLA, Omar (Argentina – dates unknown)

Requiem for a Woman's Soul – Fiction. Trans. Paul Riviera and author. Random House: New York, 1986; Penguin Books: Harmondsworth, 1987.

RIVERA, José Eustacio (Colombia 1889–1928)

The Vortex – Fiction. Trans. Earle K. James. Putnam: New York, 1935. *La vorágine*, 1924.

ROA BASTOS, Augusto (Paraguay 1917–)

Son of Man – Fiction. Trans. Rachel Caffyn. Gollancz: London, 1965. *Hijo de hombre*, 1961.

I the Supreme – Fiction. Trans. Helen Lane. Knopf: New York, 1986; Faber & Faber: London, 1987. *Yo el supremo*, 1974.

ROJAS, Manuel (Chile 1896–1973)

Born Guilty – Fiction. Trans. Frank Gaynor. Library Publishers: New York, 1955; Gollancz: London, 1956. *Hijo de ladrón*, 1951.

ROMERO, José Rubén (Mexico 1890–1952)

The Futile Life of Pito Pérez – Fiction. Trans. W. Cord. J. Coyne: Englewoods Cliffs, NJ, 1966. *La vida inútil de Pito Pérez*, 1938.

ROSA, João Guimarães (Brazil 1908–67)

The Devil to Pay in the Backlands – Fiction. Trans. J. L. Taylor and Harriet de Onís. Knopf: New York, 1963. *Grande Sertão: Veredas*, 1956.

Sagarana – Fiction. Trans. Harriet de Onís. Knopf: New York, 1958. *Sagarana*, 1946.

The Third Bank of the River and Other Stories – Fiction. Trans. Barbara Shelby. Knopf: New York, 1968. *Primeiras estórias*, 1962.

ROSSI, Cristina Peri (Uruguay 1941–)

The Ship of Fools – Fiction. Trans. Psiche Hughes. Allison & Busby: London, 1989. *La nave de los locos*, 1984.

RUBIÃO, Murilo (Brazil 1916–)

The Ex-Magician and Other Stories – Fiction. Trans. Thomas Colchie. Harper & Row: New York, 1979. *Os dragões e outros contos*, 1965.

RUGAMA, Leonel (Nicaragua 1950–70)

The Earth is a Satellite of the Moon – Poetry. Trans. Sara Miles, Richard Schaaf, Nancy Weisberg. Curbstone Press: Willimantic, Conn., 1985.

RULFO, Juan (Mexico 1918–86)

Pedro Paramo, a Novel of Mexico – Fiction. Trans. Lysander Kemp. Grove Press: New York, 1959; John Calder: London, 1959. *Pedro Páramo*, 1955.

The Burning Plain and Other Stories – Fiction. Trans. George D. Schade. Univ. of Texas Press: Austin, 1967. *El llano en llamas*, 1953.

S

SÁBATO, Ernesto (Argentina 1911–)

The Outsider – Fiction. Trans. Harriet de Onís. Knopf: New York, 1950. *El túnel*, 1948.

On Heroes and Tombs – Fiction. Trans. Helen Lane. Godine: Boston, 1981; Cape: London, 1982. *Sobre héroes y tumbas*, 1961.

The Tunnel – Fiction. Trans. Margaret Sayers Peden. Random House: New York, 1988; Cape: London, 1988. *El túnel*, 1948.

SABINES, Jaime (Mexico 1926–)

Tarumba: Selected Poems of Jaime Sabines – Poetry. Trans. Philip Levine and Ernesto Trejo. Twin Peeks Press: Portland, Ore., 1975.

SABINO, Fernando (Brazil 1923–)

A Time to Meet – Fiction. Trans. John Procter. Souvenir Press: London, 1967; Panther Books: London, 1968. *O encontro marcado*, 1956.

SÁINZ, Gustavo (Mexico 1940–)

Gazapo – Fiction. Trans. Hardie St. Martin. Farrar, Straus & Giroux: New York, 1968. *Gazapo*, 1965.

The Princess of the Iron Palace – Fiction. Trans. Andrew Hurley. Grove Press: New York, 1987. *La princesa del Palacio de Hierro*, 1974.

SALES, Heberto (Brazil 1917–)

The Werewolf and Other Stories – Fiction. Trans. Richard Goddard. Rex Collings: London, 1978. *O lobisomem e outros contos folclóricos*, 1970.

The Fruit of Thy Womb – Fiction. Trans. Michael Fody III. Wyvern: Bringsty, Worcs., 1982. *O fruto do vosso ventre*, 1976.

SÁNCHEZ, Florencio (Uruguay 1875-1910)

Representative Plays of Florencio Sánchez – Theatre. Trans. & ed. Willis Knapp Jones. Pan American Union: Washington, DC, 1961. *M'Hijo el dotor*, 1903; *La gringa*, 1904.

SÁNCHEZ, Luis Rafael (Puerto Rico 1936–)

Macho Camacho's Beat – Fiction. Pantheon: New York, 1981; Avon Books: New York, 1982. *La guaracha del macho Camacho*, 1976.

SARDUY, Severo (Cuba 1937–)

From Cuba with a Song, in *Triple Cross* – Fiction. Trans. Suzanne Jill Levine. Dutton: New York, 1973. *¿De dónde son los cantantes?* 1965.

Cobra – Fiction. Trans. Suzanne Jill Levine. Dutton: New York, 1975. *Cobra*, 1973.

For Voice – Theatre/poetry. Trans. Philip Barnard. Latin American Literary Review Press: Pittsburgh, 1985. *Para la voz*, 1977.

Maitreya – Fiction. Trans. Suzanne Jill Levine. Ediciones del Norte: Hanover, NH, 1987. *Maitreya*, 1978.

SARNEY, José (Brazil 1931–)

Tales of Rain and Sunlight – Fiction. Wyvern-Sel: Bringsty, Worcs., 1986. *Noites das águas*, 1969.

SATZ, Mario (Argentina 1944–)

Sol – Fiction. Trans. Helen Lane. Doubleday: New York, 1979; Sidgwick & Jackson: London, 1979. *Sol*, 1976.

SCHIZMAN, Mario (Argentina 1945–)

At 8.25 Evita became Immortal – Fiction. Trans. Roberto Piccioto. Ediciones del Norte: Hanover, NH, 1983. *A las 20.25 la señora entró en la inmortalidad*, 1981.

SCLIAR, Moacyr (Brazil 1937–)

The Gods of Raquel – Fiction. 1986 (other publication details unknown). *Os deuses de Raquel*, 1975.

The One-Man Army – Fiction. Ballantine: New York, 1986. *O exército de um homem só*, 1973.

The Centaur in the Garden – Fiction. Trans. Margaret A. Neves. Available Press: New York, 1984. *O centauro no jardim*, 1980.

The Carnival of the Animals – Fiction. Trans. Eloh F. Giacomelli. Ballantine: New York, 1985. *O carnaval dos animais*, 1968.

The Battle of the False Messiah – Fiction. Ballantine: New York, 1987. Title and date of original unknown.

The Strange Nation of Rafael Mendés – Fiction. Trans. Eloah F. Giacomelli. Harmony Books: New York, 1988. *A estranha nação de Rafael Mendés*, 1983.

SCORZA, Manuel (Peru 1928–83)

Drums for Rancas – Fiction. Trans. Edith Grossman. Harper & Row: New York, 1977; Secker & Warburg: London, 1977. *Redoble por Rancas*, 1970.

SEIXAS FRAGA, Cid (Brazil 1948–)

O Signo selvagem. The Savage Sign – Poetry. Trans. H. Fox and B. Machado Costa. Ghost Dance Press: East Lancing, Mich., 1981. *O Signo selvagem*, date unknown.

SILVEIRA de QUEIROZ, Dinah (Brazil 1910–83)

Christ's Memorial – Fiction. Trans. Isabel do Prado. Sel Press: London, 1978. *Eu, venho*, 1974.

The Women of Brazil – Fiction. Trans. Roberta King. Vantage Press: New York, 1980. Title and date of original unknown.

SKÁRMETA, Antonio (Chile 1940–)

The Insurrection – Fiction. Trans. Paula Sharp. Ediciones del Norte: Hanover, NH, 1983. *La insurrección*, 1983.

I Dreamt the Snow was Burning – Fiction. Trans. Malcolm Coad. Readers International: London, 1985. *Soñé que la nieve ardía*, 1975.

Burning Patience – Fiction. Trans. Katherine Silver. Pantheon Books: New York, 1987; Methuen: London, 1988. *Ardiente paciencia*, 1985.

SORIANO, Osvaldo (Argentina 1943–)

A Funny Dirty Little War – Fiction. Trans. Nick Caistor. Readers International: London, 1983. *No habrá más pena ni olvido*, 1982.

SORRENTINO, Fernando (Argentina 1942–)

Sanitary Centennial and Selected Short Stories – Fiction. Trans. Thomas C. Meehan. Univ. of Texas Press: Austin, 1988. *Sanitarios centenarios*, 1979.

SOSA, Roberto (Honduras 1930–)

The Difficult Days – Poetry. Bilingual. Trans. Jim Lindsey. Introduction: two interviews with Roberto Sosa. Princeton Univ. Press: Princeton, 1983. *Los pobres*, 1967 and *Un mundo para todos dividido*, 1971.

SOTO, Pedro Juan (Puerto Rico 1928–)

Hot Land, Cold Season – Fiction. Trans. Helen Lane. Dell: New York, 1973. *Ardiente suelo, fría estación*, 1961.

Spiks – Fiction. Trans. Victoria Ortiz. Monthly Review Press: New York, 1973. *Spiks*, 1956.

SOUZA, Márcio (Brazil 1946–)

The Emperor of the Amazon – Fiction. Trans. Thomas Colchie. Avon Books: New York, 1977; Sphere Books: London, 1982. *Galvez, imperador do Acre*, 1976.

Mad Maria – Fiction. Trans. Thomas Colchie. Avon Books: New York, 1985. *Mad Maria*, 1980.

The Order of the Day. An Unidentified Flying Opus – Fiction. Trans. Thomas Colchie. Avon Books: New York, 1986. *A ordem do dia*, 1983.

SPOTA, Luis (Mexico 1925–85)

The Wounds of Hunger – Fiction. Trans. & ed. Barnaby Conrad. Houghton-Mifflin: Boston, 1957. *Más cornadas da el hambre*, 1951.

The Enemy Blood – Fiction. Trans. Robert Malloy. Doubleday: Garden City, NY, 1961; Frederick Muller: London, 1961; Penguin Books, Harmondsworth, 1967. *La sangre enemiga*, 1959.

The Time of Wrath – Fiction. Trans. Robert Malloy. Doubleday: Garden City, NY, 1962. *El tiempo de la ira*, 1960.

Almost Paradise – Fiction. Trans. Roy and Renate Morrison. Doubleday: Garden City, NY, 1963. *Casi el paraíso*, 1956.

STORNI, Alfonsina (Switzerland/Argentina 1892–1938)

Alfonsina Storni: Argentina's Feminist Poet. The Poetry in Spanish with English Translations – Poetry. Ed. Florence Williams Talamantes. San Marcos: Los Cerillos, NMex., 1975.

Selected Poems – Poetry. Trans. Dorothy Scott Loos. Amana Books: Brentwood, Md., 1986.

Selected Poems – Poetry. Trans. Marion Freeman, Mary Crow, Jim Normington and Kay Short. Ed. Marion Freeman. White Pine Press: New York, 1987.

SUBERCASEAUX, Benjamín (Chile 1902–73).

From West to East: Five Stories – Fiction. Trans. & ed. John Underhill. Putnam: New York, 1940. *Y al oeste limita con el mar*, 1937 and *Rahab*, 1938.

Jemmy Button – Fiction. Trans. Mary and Fred del Villar. Macmillan: New York, 1954; W. H. Allen: London, 1955. *Jemmy Button*, 1950.

T

TAUNY, Viscount A. d'e (Brazil 1843–99)

Inocência – Fiction. Trans. Henriqueta Chamberlain. Macmillan: New York, 1945. *Inocência*, 1872.

TELLES, Lygia Fagundes (Brazil 1923–)

The Girl in the Photograph – Fiction. Trans. Margaret A. Neves. Avon Books: New York, 1982. *As meninas*, 1973.

The Marble Dance – Fiction. Trans. Margaret A. Neves. Avon Books: New York, 1986. *Ciranda de pedra*, 1954.

Tigrela and Other Stories – Fiction. Trans. Margaret A. Neves. Avon Books: New York, 1986. *Seminário dos ratos*, 1977.

TORRES, Antônio (Brazil 1940–)

The Land – Fiction. Trans. Margaret A. Neves. Readers International: London, 1987. *Essa terra*, 1976.

TORRES BODET, Jaime (Mexico 1902–74)

Selected Poems – Poetry. Bilingual. Trans. Sonja Karsen. Indiana Univ. Press: Bloomington, 1964.

TRABA, Marta (Argentina 1930–85)

Mothers and Shadows – Fiction. Trans. Jo Labanyi. Readers International: London, 1986. *Conversación al sur*, 1981.

TREVISAN, Dalton (Brazil 1925–)

The Vampires of Curitiba and Other Stories – Fiction. Trans. Gregory Rabassa. Knopf: New York, 1972. *O vampiro de Curitiba*, 1965.

U

USIGLI, Rodolfo (Mexico 1905–)

Crown of Shadows – Theatre. Trans. William Stirling. Wingate: London, 1946. *Corona de sombra*, 1943.

Two Plays. Crown of Light & One of These Days – Theatre. Trans. Thomas Bledsoe. Southern Illinois Univ. Press: Carbondale, 1971. *Corona de luz*, 1965.

USLAR PIETRI, Arturo (Venezuela 1906–)

The Red Lances – Fiction. Trans. Harriet de Onís. Knopf: New York, 1963. *Las lanzas coloradas*, 1931.

V

VACANO, Arturo von (Bolivia 1938–)

Biting Silence – Fiction. Avon Books: New York, 1987. Title and date of original unknown.

VALDELOMAR, Abraham (Peru 1888–1919)

Our Children of the Sun. A Suite of Inca Legends from Peru – Fiction. Southern Illinois Univ. Press: Carbondale, 1968. *Los hijos del sol*, 1920.

VALDIVIESO, Mercedes – pseud. for Mercedes Valenzuela Alvarez (Chile 1925–65)

Breakthrough (La brecha)–Fiction. Trans. Graciela Daichman. Latin American Literary Review Press: Pittsburgh, 1987. *La brecha*, 1961.

VALENZUELA, Luisa (Argentina 1938–)

Clara; Thirteen Short Stories and a Novel – Fiction. Trans. Hortense Carpentier and Jorge Castello. Harcourt Brace Jovanovich: New York, 1976. *Hay que sonreír*, 1966 and *Los heréticos*, 1967.

Strange Things Happen here – Fiction. Trans. Helen Lane. Harcourt Brace Jovanovich: New York, 1979. *Aquí pasan cosas raras*, 1975.

The Lizard's Tale – Fiction. Trans. Gregory Rabassa. Farrar, Straus & Giroux: New York, 1983; Serpent's Tail: London, 1987. *Cola de lagartija*, 1983.

Other Weapons – Fiction. Trans. Deborah Bonner. Ediciones del Norte: Hanover, NH, 1985. *Cambio de armas*, 1982.

Up Among the Eagles – Fiction. North Point Press: Berkeley, Calif., 1988. Title and date of original unknown.

Open Door – Fiction (Anthology). Trans. Hortense Carpentier, J. Jorge Castello, Helen Lane, Christopher Leland, Margaret Sayers Peden and David Unger. North Point Press: Berkeley, Calif., 1988.

VALLE, Rosamel del (Chile 1900–63)

Journey to Bear Mountain – Poetry. Bilingual. Trans. José Vázquez Amaral. Oasis: Toronto, 1975.

VALLEJO, César (Peru 1892–1938)

Twenty Poems of César Vallejo – Poetry. Bilingual. Trans. John Knoepfle, James Wright and Robert Bly. Sixties Press: Maddison, Minn., 1967.

Poemas humanos, Human Poems – Poetry. Bilingual. Trans. Clayton Eshelman. Grove Press: New York, 1968. *Poemas humanos*, 1938.

Ten Versions from Trilce – Poetry. Trans. Charles Tomlinson and Henry Gifford. San Marcos Press: New Mexico, 1970. *Trilce*, 1922.

Neruda and Vallejo: Selected Poems – Poetry. Bilingual. Ed. Robert Bly. Trans. Robert Bly, John Knoepfle and James Wright. Beacon Press: Boston, 1972.

Trilce – Poetry. Bilingual. Trans. David Smith. Grossman: New York, 1973. *Trilce*. 1922.

Spain, Take this Cup from Me – Poetry. Trans. Clayton Eshelman and José Rubia Barcia. Grove Press: New York, 1974. *España, aparta de mí este cáliz*, 1940.

Selected Poems – Poetry. Bilingual. Trans., sel. & ed. Ed Dorn and Gordon Brotherston. Penguin Books: Harmondsworth, 1976.

Spain, Let this Cup pass from me – Poetry. Trans. Alvaro Cardona-Hine. Red Hill Press: Fairfax, Calif., 1977. *España, aparta de mí este cáliz*, 1940.

The Complete Posthumous Poetry – Poetry. Trans. Clayton Eshelman and José Rubia Barcia. Univ. of California Press: Berkeley & Los Angeles, 1978.

Songs of my Home – Poetry. Zeilig Bros: U.S.A., 1981. *Canciones de hogar*, 1919.

Selected Poems – Poetry. Bilingual. Trans. H. R. Hays. Sachem Press: New York, 1981.

Palms and Guitar – Poetry. Trans. J. C. R. Greene. Aquila Publishing Co.: Isle of Skye, 1982.

Autopsy on Surrealism – Essay. Trans. R. Schaaf. Curbstone Press: Willimantic, Conn., 1986.

Mayakovsky Case – Essay. Trans. R. Schaaf. Curbstone Press: Willimantic, Conn., 1986.

César Vallejo. A Selection of his Poetry – Poetry. Trans., introd., & notes. James Higgins. Francis Cairns: Liverpool, 1987.

Tungsten: a Novel – Fiction. Trans. Robert Mezey. Syracuse Univ. Press: Syracuse, 1988. *El tungsteno*, 1931.

VARGAS LLOSA, Mario (Peru 1936–)

The Time of the Hero – Fiction. Trans. Lysander Kemp. Grove Press: New York, 1966; Penguin Books: Harmondsworth, 1966; Cape: London, 1967; Picador: London, 1986. *La ciudad y los perros*, 1962.

The Green House – Fiction. Trans. Gregory Rabassa. Harper & Row: New York, 1968; Cape: London, 1969; Picador: London, 1986. *La casa verde*, 1965.

Conversation in the Cathedral – Fiction. Trans. Gregory Rabassa. Harper & Row: New York, 1975. *Conversación en la catedral*, 1970.

Captain Pantoja and the Special Service – Fiction. Trans. Gregory Kolovakos and Ronald Christ. Harper & Row: New York, 1978; Cape: London, 1978; Faber & Faber: London, 1987. *Pantaleón y las visitadoras*, 1973.

The Cubs and Other Stories – Fiction. Trans. Ronald Christ and Gregory Kolovakos. Harper & Row: New York, 1980. *Los cachorros*, 1967.

Aunt Julia and the Script Writer – Fiction. Trans. Helen Lane. Farrar, Straus & Giroux: New York, 1982; Faber & Faber: London, 1983; Picador: London, 1984. *La tía Julia y el escribidor*, 1977.

The War of the End of the World – Fiction. Trans. Helen Lane. Farrar, Straus & Giroux: New York, 1984; Faber & Faber: London, 1985. *La Guerra del fin del mundo*, 1981.

The Real Life of Alejandro Mayta – Fiction. Trans. Alfred MacAdam. Farrar, Straus & Giroux: New York, 1986; Faber & Faber: London, 1986. *Historia de Mayta*, 1984.

The Perpetual Orgy – Essay. Trans. Helen Lane. Farrar, Straus & Giroux: New York, 1986; Faber & Faber: London, 1987. *La orgía perpetua: Flaubert y Madame Bovary*, 1975.

Who Killed Palomino Molero? – Fiction. Trans. Alfred MacAdam. Farrar, Straus & Giroux: New York, 1987; Faber & Faber: London, 1988. *¿Quién mató a Palomino Molero?* 1986.

VASCONCELOS, José Mauro de (Brazil 1920–84)

My Sweet-Orange Tree – Fiction. Trans. Edgar H. Miller Jr. Knopf: New York, 1970; Michael Joseph: London, 1971; Hutchinson: London, 1983. *Meu pé de lavanga lima*, 1968.

VEIGA, José (Brazil 1915–)

The Misplaced Machine and Other Stories – Fiction. Trans. Pamela G. Bird. Knopf: New York, 1970. *A máquina extraviada*, 1968.

The Three Trials of Manirema – Fiction. Trans. Pamela G. Bird. Knopf: New York, 1970; Peter Owen: London, 1979. *A hora dos rumiantes*, 1966.

VERÍSIMO, Eric (Brazil 1905–75)

Crossroads – Fiction. Trans. L. C. Kaplan. Macmillan: New York, 1943; publ. as *Crossroads and Destinies*. Arco: London, 1956; Greenwood Press: New York, 1969. *Caminhos cruzados*, 1935.

The Rest is Silence – Fiction. Trans. L. C. Kaplan. Macmillan: New York, 1946; Arco: London, 1956. *O resto é silencio*, 1943.

Consider the Lilies of the Field – Fiction. Trans. Jean Karnoff. Macmillan: New York, 1947; Greenwood Press: New York, 1969. *Olhai os lírios do campo*, 1938.

Time and the Wind – Fiction. Trans. Linton Barrett. Macmillan: New York, 1951; Arco: London, 1954. *O tempo e o vento*, 1949.

Night – Fiction. Trans. Linton Barrett. Macmillan: New York, 1956; Arco: London, 1956. *Noite*, 1954.

His Excellency, the Ambassador – Fiction. Trans. Linton Barrett and Marie Barrett. Macmillan: New York, 1967. *O Senhor embaixador*, 1965.

VIERCI, Pablo (Uruguay 1950–)

The Impostors: the Truth and the Lies about their Travels through the Amazon – Fiction. Trans. Sara Nelson. Avon Books: New York, 1987. Title and date of original unknown.

VILLAVERDE, Cirilo (Cuba 1812–94)

The Quadroon or Cecilia Valdés – Fiction. Trans. Mariano J. Lorente. Farrar, Straus & Giroux: New York, 1935. *Cecilia Valdés o la loma del ángel*, 1882.

Cecilia Valdés; a Novel of Cuban Customs – Fiction. Trans. Sydney G. Gest. Vantage Press: New York, 1962. *Cecilia Valdés o la loma del ángel*, 1882.

WYZ

WOLFF, Egon (Chile 1926–)

Paper Flowers – Theatre. Trans. Margaret Sayers Peden. Univ. of Missouri Press: Columbia, 1971. *Flores de papel*, 1968.

YÁÑEZ, Agustín (Mexico 1904–80)

The Edge of the Storm – Fiction. Trans. Ethel Brinton. Univ. of Texas Press: Austin, 1963. *Al filo del agua*, 1947.

The Lean Lands – Fiction. Trans. Ethel Brinton. Univ. of Texas Press: Austin, 1968. *Las tierras flacas*, 1962.

ZORILLA de SAN MARTÍN, Juan (Uruguay 1855–1931)

Tabaré: an Indian Legend of Uruguay – Poetry. Trans. Walter Owen. Pan American Union: Washington, DC, 1956. *Tabaré*, 1879.

ZURITA, Raúl (Chile 1951–)

Purgatorio 1970–1977 – Poetry. Trans. Jeremy Jacobson. Latin American Literary Review Press: Pittsburgh, 1985. *Purgatorio*, 1977.

Anteparadise – Poetry. Trans. Jack Schmidt. Univ. of California Press: Berkeley & Los Angeles, 1987. *Anteparaíso*, 1982.

ANTHOLOGIES
in chronological order of publication.

1920

Brazilian Tales. Trans. & ed. Isaac Goldberg. The Four Seas Co: Boston, 1921; Knopf: New York, 1924; International Pocket Library: Boston, 1965.

Some Spanish-American Poets. Bilingual. Trans. Alice Stone Blackwell. Introd. & notes Isaac Goldberg. Appleton & Co.: New York, 1929. Includes Nervo, Díaz Mirón, Darío, Lugones etc.

1930

Tales from the Argentine. Ed. Waldo Frank. Trans. Anita Brenner. Farrar & Rinehart: New York, 1930. Includes Güiraldes, Lugones, Quiroga, Sarmiento etc.

Anthology of Mexican Poets: From the Earliest Times to the Present Day. Trans. Edna Worthley Underwood. The Mosher Press: Portland, Ore., 1932. Includes Villaurrutia, Novo, López Velarde, Nervo, Sor Juana etc.

The Modernist Trend in Spanish American Poetry. Trans. & comp. George D. Craig. Univ. of California Press: Berkeley, 1934. Includes Banchs, Huidobro, Neruda, Mistral, Storni, Silva, Borges, Lugones etc.

1940

Anthology of Contemporary Latin-American Poetry. Bilingual. Ed. Dudley Fitts. New Directions: Norfolk, Conn., 1942. Includes Carrera Andrade, Gorostiza, Florit, Mistral, Borges, Torres Bodet, Palés Matos, Guillén, Neruda, Pellicer, Oquendo de Amat, Huidobro, Villaurrutia, Abril, Moro, Bandeira, Mendes, de Lima and many others.

Fiesta in November; Stories from Latin America. Eds. Angel Flores and Dudley Poore. Trans. Harriet de Onís, de Sola, Flores and others.

Houghton Mifflin: Boston, 1942. Includes Jorge Amado, Barrios, Mallea, Quiroga, Aguilar Malta etc.

Three Spanish-American Poets: Pellicer, Neruda, Andrade. Trans. & ed. Lloyd Mallan. Swallow & Critchlow: Albuquerque, NMex., 1942.

Argentine Anthology of Modern Verse. Trans. & eds. Patricio Gannon and Hugo Manning. Francisco Columbo: Buenos Aires, 1942.

Twelve Spanish American Poets: an Anthology. Bilingual. Ed. H. R. Hays. Yale Univ. Press: New Haven, 1943; Beacon Press: Boston, 1972. López Velarde, Gorostiza, López, Neruda, Rokha, Huidobro, Florit, Guillén, Borges, Carrera Andrade, Vallejo and Fombona Pachano.

The Green Continent. Sel. & ed. Germán Arciniegas. Trans. Harriet de Onís. Editions Poetry London: London, 1947.

The Golden Land; an Anthology of Latin American Folklore. Trans. & ed. Harriet de Onís. Knopf: New York, 1948. Includes Borges, Guzmán, Alcides Arguedas, Güiraldes etc.

Argentine Anthology. Comp. by S. W. de Ferdkin, with Elizabeth Dall, Robin Clarke de Armando, Charles Yates. Oxford Univ. Press: London, 1948. Includes Rojas, Sarmiento, Mitre, Cané, Güiraldes and Wilde.

1950

Spanish Stories and Tales. Ed. Harriet de Onís. Trans. Onís, Howard Young and others. Knopf: New York, 1954. Includes Borges, Gallegos, Güiraldes, Mallea, Quiroga etc.

An introduction to Modern Brazilian Poetry; Verse Translations. Trans. Leonard Downes. Club de Poesia do Brasil: São Paulo, 1954.

Modern Poetry from Brazil. Bilingual. Dolphin Book Co: Cambridge, 1955. Includes Mario de Andrade, Bandeira, Lima, Meireles etc.

Swans, Cygnets and Owls: an Anthology of Modernist Poetry in Spanish America. Trans. & ed. Mildred Johnson. The Univ. of Missouri Studies: Columbia, 1956. Includes Agustini, Borges, Casal, Darío, Nájera, Martí, Neruda, Bodet etc.

Contistas brasileiros; New Brazilian Short Stories. Ed. José Saldanha da Gama Coelho Pinto. Trans. Rod. W. Horton. Revista Branca: Rio de Janeiro, 1957.

UNESCO Anthology of Mexican Poetry. Trans. Samuel Beckett. Introd. Octavio Paz. Univ. of Indiana Press: Bloomington, 1958; Thames & Hudson: London, 1958; Calder & Boyars: London, 1970. Includes Sor

Juana, Othón, Nervo, Tablada, López Velarde etc.

"The Eye of Mexico", **Evergreen Review**, no.7, Winter 1959. Trans. Paul Blackburn, Lysander Kemp and others. Includes Rulfo, Garro, Fuentes, Pozas, Arreola, Paz, Chumacero, Sabines, Durán, Montes de Oca, García Terrés.

1960

Spanish Stories/ Cuentos hispánicos. Trans. & ed. Angel Flores. Bantam: New York, 1960. Includes Palma, Quiroga, Lynch and Borges.

Poetisas de América. Trans. & ed. Helen Wohl Paterson. Mitchell Press: Washington, 1960.

New Voices of Hispanic America. An Anthology. Bilingual. Trans. & ed. Darwin J. Flakoll and Claribel Alegría. Beacon Press: Boston, 1962. Includes Blanca Varela, Cardenal, Pasos, Vitier, Gonzalo Rojas, Paz, Anguita, Parra, Lihn, Rulfo, Monterroso, Murena, Arreola, Cortázar and many others.

Classic Tales from Spanish America. Trans. & ed. William Colford. Barron: Woodbury, NY, 1962. Includes Manuel Rojas, Lugones, Uslar Pietri etc.

Spanish American Literature in Translation. Ed. Willis Knapp Jones. Frederick Ungar: New York, 1963. Vol. 1 up to 1888; Vol. 2 since 1888.

Short Stories of Latin America. Ed. Arturo Torres-Ríoseco. Trans. Ziola Nelken and Rosalie Torres-Ríoseco. Las Américas: New York, 1963.

Prize Stories from Latin America. Pref. Arturo Uslar Pietri. Trans. Paul Blackburn, Lysander Kemp, Harriet de Onís, Jerome Rothenberg and others. Doubleday: New York, 1964. Includes Conti, Denevi, Martínez Moreno etc.

Modern Poetry from Spain and Latin America. Trans. Nan Braymer and Lillian Lowenfels. Corinth Books: New York, 1964.

From the Green Antilles. Ed. Barbara Howes. Macmillan: New York, 1966. Includes Bosch, Lydia Cabrera, Carpentier.

Caribbean Literature. An Anthology. Trans., sel. & ed. G. R. Coulthard. Univ. of London Press: London, 1966. Includes Guillén, Palés Matos.

Short Stories in Spanish. Cuentos hispánicos. Ed. Jean Franco. Trans. Donald Yates, Gerald Brown, Gordon Brotherston, Richard Southern, Donald Shaw, Giovanni Pontiero, Janet Chapman. Penguin Books: Harmondsworth, 1966. Includes Borges, Onetti, Murena, Martínez Moreno, Rulfo, Benedetti.

Writers in the New Cuba. An Anthology. Ed. J. M. Cohen. Trans. J. M. Cohen, Gordon Brotherston, Jean Franco. Penguin Books: Harmondsworth, 1967. Includes Padilla, Piñera, Cabrera Infante, Arenal and 18 others.

Cuban Poetry, 1959-1966. Bilingual. Ed. Heberto Padilla and Luis Suardíaz. Instituto del Libro: Havana, 1967.

Young Poetry of the Americas. General Secretariat of the OAS: Washington, DC, 1967.

Modern Brazilian Short Stories. Trans. & ed. William Grossman. Univ. of California Press: Berkeley & Los Angeles, 1967.

Cuban Short Stories 1959-1966. Eds. Sylvia Carranza and María Juana Cazabon. Book Institute: Havana, 1967.

Modern Brazilian Poetry. Ed. and trans. John Nist. Univ. of Texas Press: Austin, 1967.

Latin American Writing Today. Ed. J. M. Cohen. Trans. J. M. Cohen, Charles Tomlinson, Doris Dana, Jean Franco, Gordon Brotherston and others. Penguin Books: Harmondsworth, 1967. Includes Fuentes, Vargas Llosa, Benedetti, Cabrera Infante, Paz, Sabines, Vallejo, Molinari, Neruda, Drummond de Andrade, Parra, Girri, Lihn and others.

'Contemporary Latin American Literature', in **Triquarterly**, 13/14, Fall/Winter 1968/69, guest co-ed. José Donoso. Reprinted as **The Triquarterly Anthology of Contemporary Latin American Literature**. Ed. José Donoso and William A. Henkin. Dutton: New York, 1969. Includes Paz, Sábato, Sáinz, Arreola, García Márquez, Borges, Trevisan, Donoso, Leñero, Asturias, Edwards, Vallejo, Molina, Belli, Neruda, Lihn, Parra and many others.

Chile: an Anthology of New Writing. Trans. & ed. Miller Williams. Kent State University Press: Kent, 1968.

Nine Latin American Poets. Bilingual. Trans. & ed. Ruth Benson. Las Américas: New York, 1968. Includes Gorostiza, Huidobro, Neruda, Palés Matos, Paz, Pellicer, Storni, Vallejo and Villaurrutia.

Our Word. Guerrilla Poems from Latin America. Bilingual. Trans. & ed. Ed Dorn and Gordon Brotherston. Cape Goliard: London, 1968.

Contemporary Argentine Poetry. Comp. & trans. William Shand. Introd. Aldo Pellegrini. Fundación Argentina para la Poesía: Buenos Aires, 1969. Includes Aguirre, Alonso, Armani, Bayley, Borges, Bustos, Ceselli, Gelman, Girri, Juarroz, Latorre, Llinás, Madariaga, Molina, Molinari, Pizarnik, Pellegrini and many others.

Con Cuba. An Anthology of Cuban Poetry of the last 60 Years. Ed. Nathaniel Tarn. Trans. Nathaniel Tarn, Tom Raworth, Tim Reynolds, Adrian Mitchell, Donald Gardner, Anthony Kerrigan. Cape: London, 1969; Grossman: New York, 1969. Includes Lezama Lima, Diego, Vitier, Jamís, Retamar, Padilla, Morejón and 23 others.

'Special Spanish-American Poetry Issue'. **Mundus Artium**, Winter 1969, guest ed. Sergio Mondragón. Includes Juarroz, Molina, Pizarnik, Lihn, Paz, Huidobro, Lezama Lima, Vitier, Cardenal, Sabines, Blanca Varela, Zaid, Fraile, Pacheco, Aridjis.

Unstill Life. Naturaleza viva: an Introduction to the Spanish Poetry of Latin America. Trans. Claribel Alegría and Darwin J. Flakoll. Ed. & introd. Mario Benedetti. Harcourt Brace & World: New York, 1969. Includes Vallejo, Darío, Neruda, Paz, Sabines, Gelman, Montes de Oca, Parra, Huidobro etc.

1970

New Poetry of Mexico. Bilingual. Ed. Mark Strand. Trans. Strand, Donald Justice and others. Dutton: New York, 1970; Secker & Warburg: London, 1972. **Poesía en movimiento**, eds. Octavio Paz, José Emilio Pacheco, Homero Aridjis and Alí Chumacero, 1966.

Peru: the New Poetry. Eds. Maureen Ahern and David Tipton. Trans. Ahern, Tipton and William Rowe. London Magazine Editions: London, 1970. Poets include Salazar Bondy, Washington Delgado, Germán Belli, Guevara, Hinostroza, Cisneros, Heraud, Ortega and Lauer. 2nd. ed. Red Dust: New York, 1977 with new poems and poets (Sologuren, Bustamante and Sánchez León).

Men and Angels. Three South American Comedies. Trans., introd. & ed. Willis Knapp Jones. Southern Illinois Univ. Press: Carbondale, 1970. Includes Rivarola, Matto, Frank etc.

Tales of Love, Fantasy and Horror; a Taste of Poe in the Spanish American Short Story. Trans. R. C. Peterson. Exposition Press: New York, 1971.

The Penguin Book of Latin American Verse. Ed. Enrique Caracciolo-Trejo. Penguin Books: Harmondsworth, 1971.

Voices of Change in the Spanish American Theater. An Anthology. Trans., ed. & introd. William Oliver. Univ. of Texas Press: Austin, 1971. Includes Carballido, Gambero, Maggi, Vodánovic etc.

The Modern Stage in Latin America: Six Plays; An Anthology. Trans. & ed. George Woodyard. Dutton: New York, 1971. Includes Marqués, Dragún, Díaz, Triana, Carballido etc.,

Latin Blood: the Best Crime and Detective Stories of South America. Ed. Donald Yates. Herder & Herder: New York, 1972.

The Eye of the Heart. Ed. Barbara Howes. Bobbs-Merril: New York, 1972; Allison & Busby: London, 1987; W. H. Allen: London, 1988. Includes Borges, Asturias, Paz, Quiroga, Cortázar, García Márquez, Vargas Llosa.

The Puerto Rican Poets: Los poetas puertorriqueños. Bilingual. Ed. Alfredo Matilla and Iván Silén. Bantam: New York, 1972.

An Anthology of Twentieth Century Brazilian Literature. Bilingual. Eds. Elizabeth Bishop and Emanuel Brasil. Wesleyan Univ. Press: Middletown, 1972. Includes Bandeira, de Lima, de Andrade, Drummond de Andrade etc.

Poesia brasileira moderna. A Bilingual Anthology. Ed. Jose Neistein. Trans. Manuel Cardoso. Brazilian-American Cultural Institute: Washington, 1972.

Doors and Mirrors: Fiction and Poetry from Spanish America (1920-1970). Ed. Hortense Carpentier and Janet Brof. Viking Press: New York, 1973.

Selected Latin American One Act Plays. Ed. & trans. Francesca Colecchia and Julio Matas. Univ. of Pittsburgh Press: Pittsburgh, 1973. Includes Solórzano, Jorge Díaz.

Contemporary Latin American Short Stories. Ed. Pat McNees Mancini. Fawcett: Greenwich, Conn., 1974.

Latin American Revolutionary Poetry. Poesía revolucionaria latinoamericana. Ed. & introd. Robert Márquez. Trans. Robert Márquez, Elinor Randall, David Arthur McMurray and others. Monthly Review Press: London, 1974. Includes Molina, Gelman, García Robles, Shimose, de Mello, Lihn, Guillén, Retamar and others.

The Orgy: Modern One-Act Plays from Latin America. Trans., ed. & introd. Gerardo Luzuriaga and Robert Rudder. Univ. of California Latin American Center: Los Angeles, 1974. Includes Dragún, Díaz, Denevi, Solórzano and others.

Modern Brazilian Poetry. Trans. J. C. R. Green. Aquila / Phaeton Press: Isle of Skye, 1975.

Fireflight, Poetry. Trans. Catherine Rodríguez-Nieto. Oyez Press: Kensington, Calif., 1976. Elsie Alvarado de Ricard, Lucha Corpi, Concha Michel.

The Borzoi Anthology of Latin American Literature. Ed. Emir

Rodríguez Monegal, with Thomas Colchie. Knopf: New York, 1977. 2 vols.

Latin American Literature Today. Ed. Anne Freemantle. New American Library: New York, 1977. Includes Alegría, Asturias, Borges, Cardenal, Carpentier etc.

Writing in Cuba Since the Revolution. An Anthology of Poems, Short Stories and Essays. Ed. & introd. Andrew Salkey. Several translators. Bogle-L'Ouverture: London, 1977.

Open to the Sun: a Bilingual Anthology of Latin American Women Poets. Ed. & trans. Nora Jacquez Wieser. Perivale Press: Van Nuys, Calif., 1977(?).

Beyond the Rivers: An Anthology of Twentieth Century Paraguayan Poetry. Ed. & introd. Charles Richard Carlisle. Trans. Charles Carlisle, Bruce Culter, Willis Knapp Jones, Edward James Schuster. Thorp Springs Press: Berkeley, Calif., 1977.

The Yellow Canary Whose Eye is So Black: Poems of Spanish-Speaking Latin America. Bilingual. Ed. Cheli Durán. Macmillan: New York, 1977. Includes Sor Juana, Paz, Lihn and Cisneros.

A Fist and the Letter. Revolutionary Poems of Latin America. Trans. Roger Prentice and John M. Kirk. Pulp Press: Vancouver, 1977. Includes Cardenal, Dalton, Depestre, Guillén, Huasi, Romualdo and others.

Estos cantos habitados / These Living Songs. Bilingual. Colorado State Review Press: Fort Collins, Colo., 1978.

Love Stories, a Brazilian Collection. Ed. Edla van Steen. Trans. Elizabeth Lowe. Editora Hamburg: São Paulo, 1978.

Cuentos: an Anthology of Short Stories from Puerto Rico. Ed. Kal Wagenheim. Schoken: New York, 1978. 12 stories.

An Anthology of Spanish Poetry. From the Beginnings to the Present Day including both Spain and Spanish America. Comp. & ed. John A. Crow. Trans. John Crow, Ben Belitt, Lysander Kemp, H. R. Hays, Donald Walsh and others. Lousiana State University Press: Baton Rouge, 1979. Includes Darío, López Velarde, Huidobro, Vallejo, Mistral, Neruda, Gorostiza, Carrera Andrade, Florit and Paz.

The Newest Peruvian Poetry in Translation. Bilingual. Ed. Luis A. Ramos-García and Edgar O'Hara. Several trans. Studia Hispanica Editors: Austin, Tex. 1979. Includes Sánchez León, Hinostroza, Heraud, Cisneros, Verástegui etc.

1980

The Spanish American Short Story: a Critical Anthology. Ed. Seymour Menton. Several trans. Univ. of California Press: Berkeley, 1980.

Inventing a Word. An Anthology of Twentieth-century Puerto Rican Poetry. Bilingual. Ed. & introd. Julián Marzán. Trans. Marzán, Rachel Benson, Donald Walsh, Grace Schulman. Columbia Univ. Press: New York, 1980. Includes Ribera Chevremont, Palés Matos, Julia de Burgos and 20 others.

Echad: an Anthology of Latin American Jewish Writings. Comp. Robert and Roberta Kalechofsky. Micah Publications: Marblehead, Mass., 1980.

The Plaza of Encounters. Eds. Julio Ortega and Ewing Campbell. Latitudes Press: Austin, Tex., 1981. Includes Paz, Castellanos, Sabines, Zaid, Cisneros etc.

Between Fire and Love. Contemporary Writing. Ed. Lynn A. Darrock. Various translators. Mississippi Mud: Portland, Ore., 1980.

Antología de la poesía de la mujer puertorriqueña. Anthology of Poetry by Puerto Rican Women. Bilingual. Ed. Theresa Ortiz de Hadjopoulos. Peninsula Publishing Co.: New York, 1981.

Towards an Image of Latin American Poetry. A Bilingual Anthology. Ed. & introd. Octavio Armand. Trans. Mary Barnard, Luis Harss, Thomas Hoeksema, Willis Barnstone. Logbridge-Rhodes: Durango, Colo., 1982. Includes Lezama Lima, Molina, García Vega, Liscano, Rojas, Girri, Sánchez Peláez, Mutis, Pizarnik, Sologuren.

Poets of Nicaragua. A Bilingual Anthology 1918-1979. Ed. & trans. Steven F. White. Introd. Grace Schulman. Unicorn Press: Greensboro, NC, 1982.

Breaking the Silence. Twentieth Century Poetry by Cuban Women. Bilingual. Ed. & trans. Margaret Randall. Pulp Press: Vancouver, 1982.

Chilean Writers in Exile. Ed. Fernando Alegría. Crossing Press: New York, 1982.

A South American Trilogy: Osman Lins, Felisberto Hernández and Luis Fernando Vidal. Bilingual. Trans. Fred Ellison, Ana Luiza Andrade, Stephanie Merrim, Naomi Lindstrom, Dave Oliphant. Studia Hispanica: Austin, Tex., 1982.

New Translations. Contemporary Women Authors of Latin America. Eds. Doris Meyer and Margarite Fernández Olmos. Includes stories by Castellanos, Cabrera, Garro, Bullrich and poems by Pizarnik, Varela and others. Brooklyn College Press: New York, 1983.

Brazilian Poetry, 1950-1980. Eds. Emanuel Brasil and William Jay Smith. Trans. Emanuel Brasil, William Smith, Edwin Morgan, Richard Zenith and others. Wesleyan Univ. Press: Middletown, 1983. Includes Mautier, Gullar, Haroldo and Augusto de Campos, Faustino, Pignatari and Bell.

Volcán. Poems from El Salvador, Guatemala, Honduras & Nicaragua. Bilingual. Eds. Alejandro Murgía and Barbara Paschke. Several translators. City Lights: San Francisco, 1983. Includes Dalton, Castillo, Cardenal etc.

Poetry of Transition. Mexican Poetry of 1960 and 1970. Eds. Linda Scheer and Miguel Flórez Ramírez. Trans. Linda Scheer, Michael Rieman, Brian Swann, Rochelle Cohen and others. Translation Press: Ann Arbor, Mich., 1984. Includes Becerra, Pacheco, Aridjis, Huerta, Macías and others.

'Latin America', in **Spectacular Diseases**, no. 7. Ed. Paul Buck. Trans. Paul Buck, Cola Franzen, John Lyons, Maureen Ahern, David Tipton, Linda Scheer and others. Includes Yurkievich, Perlongher, Agosín, Cobo Borda, Pacheco and others. Cambridge, 1984.

Mirrors of War. Literature and Revolution in El Salvador. Eds. Gabriela Yanes, Manuel Sorto, Horacio Castellanos Moya and Lyn Soto. Trans. Keith Ellia. Zed Books: London, 1985.

Woman who has Sprouted Wings. Poems by Contemporary Latin American Women Poets. Bilingual. Ed. Mary Crow. Trans. Mary Crow, John Felstiner, Donald Walsh, Eliot Weinberger and others. Latin American Review Press: Pittsburgh, 1984. Includes Pizarnik, Parra, Morejón, Bustamante, Jodorowsky, Alegría, Maia, Castellanos and others.

Tesserae: a Mosaic of Twentieth Century Brazilian Poetry. Ed. & trans. Charles Richard Carlisle. Latitudes Press: Fort Worth, Tex., 1984.

Other Fires: Stories from the Women of Latin America. Ed. Alberto Manguel. Trans. Alberto Manguel, Suzanne Jill Levine, William Grossman, Eloah Giacomelli, Giovanni Pontiero. Picador: London, 1986; publ. as *Other Fires: Short Fiction by Latin American Women*, Clarkson N. Potter: New York, 1986. Includes Lynch, Pizarnik, Gorodischer, Ocampo, Guido, Sommers, Arrendondo, Garro, Poniatowska, Castellanos.

Un ojo en el muro. An Eye through the Wall. Mexican Poetry 1970-1985. Bilingual. Eds. Enrique R. Lamadrid and Mario del Valle. Trans. Enrique Lamadrid, Jim Sagel, John Brandi, Ernesto Mares. Tooth of Time Books: Santa Fe, NMex., 1986. Includes Bracho, Pacheco, Aridjis and others.

Anthology of Contemporary Latin American Literature, 1960-1984. Eds. Barry J. Luby and Wayne H. Finke. Associated Univ. Presses: Toronto, 1986.

The Defiant Muse: Feminist Poems from the Middle Ages to the Present. A Bilingual Anthology. Eds. Angel Flores and Kate Flores. The Feminist Press of the City Univ. of New York: New York, 1986. Includes Sor Juana, Storni, Ibarbourou, Castellanos, Vicuña.

Poets of Chile. A Bilingual Anthology 1965-1985. Sel. & trans. Steven F. White. Unicorn Press: Greensboro, NC, 1986. 18 poets included.

'Argentine Feature Section', in **The Journal of Literary Translation**, vol. XVIII, Spring 1987. Ed. Norman Thomas di Giovanni. Trans. Norman Thomas de Giovanni, Susan Ashe, Anthony Edkins and Jason Wilson. Includes Borges, Walsh, Vanasco, Sábato, Bioy Casares, Conti, Poletti, Ulla, Guido, Constantini, Asís, Blaisten, Sorrentino, Gorodischer, Denevi, Moyano, Orgambide, Hernández, Korn, Satz, Horacio Castillo, Salas, Oteriño and others.

The Image of Black Women in Twentieth-Century South American Poetry: a Bilingual Anthology. Ed. & trans. A. V. Young. Three Continents Press: Washington, DC., 1987.

The Renewal of the Vision: Voices of Latin American Women Poets, 1940-1980. Eds. Marjorie Agosín and Cola Franzen. Spectacular Diseases: Peterborough, 1987.

The Book of Fantasy. Eds. Jorge Luis Borges, Silvina Ocampo and Adolfo Bioy-Casares. Trans. U.K. Le Guin. Xanandu: London, 1988.

Voices of Négritude, with an Anthology of Négritude Poems Translated from the French, Portuguese and Spanish. Ed. J. Finn. Quartet: London, 1988.

You Can't Drown the Fire. Latin American Women Writing in Exile. Ed. Alicia Partnoy. Trans. include Helen Lane, Elinor Randall, Margaret Randall, Magda Bogin, Eliot Weinberger. Cleis Press: Pittsburgh, 1988; Virago: London, 1989. Includes Agosín, Valenzuela, Traba, Peri Rossi, Alegría, Gambaro and others.

Women's Fiction from Latin America. Selections from Twelve Contemporary Authors. Ed. with trans. by Evelyn Picon Garfield. Wayne State Univ. Press: Detroit, 1988. Includes Cabrera, Sommers, Garro, Lispector, Gambaro, Orphée, Traba, Allende, Valenzuela etc.

Anthology of Latin American Poets in London / Antología de los poetas latinoamericanos en Londres. El Grupo de Escritores Latinoamericanos: London, 1988.

Lives on the Line. The Testimony of Contemporary Latin American Authors. Ed. with introd. Doris Meyer. Several trans. Univ. of California

Press: Berkeley, 1988. Includes Neruda, Paz, Guillén, Cortázar etc.

Reclaiming Medusa. Short Stories by Contemporary Puerto Rican Women. Trans. & ed. Diana Vélez. Spinsters/ Aunt Lute: San Francisco, 1988.

Longman Anthology of World Literature by Women, 1875-1975. Eds. Marian Arkin and Barbara Shollar. Longman: New York, 1989. Includes Agustini, Mistral, de la Parra, Storni, Ibarbourou, Cabrera, Meireles, Campobello, Bombal, de Queiroz etc.

The Nicaraguan Epic: Canto Epico to the FSLAN, and Nicaraguan Vision and other poems. Trans. Dinah Livingstone. Kantabis: London, 1989. includes Carlos Mejía Godoy, Luis Enrique Mejía Godoy and Julio Valle-Castillo.

Celeste Goes Dancing and Other Stories. An Argentine Collection. Ed. Norman Thomas di Giovanni. Trans. Norman Thomas di Giovanni and Susan Ashe. Constable: London, 1989. Ocampo, Bioy Casares, Blaisten, Sánchez Sorondo, Dos Santos, Vanasco and 7 others.

And We Sold the Rain. Contemporary Fiction from Central America. Ed. Rosario Santos. Ryan Publishing: Peterborough, 1989; Four Walls: Eight Windows: San Francisco, 1989.

Clamor of Innocence: Central American Short Stories. Eds. Barbara Paschke and David Volpendesta. City Lights: San Francisco, 1989.

Lovers and Comrades. Women's Resistance Poetry from Central America. Ed. Amanda Hopkinson. Trans. Amanda Hopkinson and members of the El Salvador Solidarity Campaign Cultural Committee. The Women's Press: London, 1989.

The Faber Book of Contemporary Latin American Short Stories. Ed. Nick Caistor. Trans. Nick Caistor, Jo Labanyi, Margaret Sayers Peden, Margaret Costa, Tricia Feeney and Cynthia Ventura. Faber & Faber: London, 1989. Includes Arias, Galeano, Onetti, Rey Rosa and 16 others.

One More Stripe to the Tiger. Ed. & trans. Sandra Reyes. Univ. of Arkansas Press: London, 1989. Includes Parra, Arteche, Donoso and other Chilean writers.

General Bibliography on Translations

Claude Hulet, *Latin American Poetry in English Translation: a Bibliography*. Pan American Union: Washington, DC, 1964.

Claude Hulet, *Latin American Prose in English Translation: a Bibliography*. Pan American Union: Washington, DC, 1964.

Suzanne Jill Levine (comp.), *Latin American Fiction and Poetry in Translation*. Center for Inter-American Relations: New York, 1970. 224 items listed.

Jean Franco (ed.), *Penguin Companion to Literature. Vol 3. Latin American Literature*. Penguin Books: Harmondsworth, 1971.

Karna S. Wilgus (ed.), *Latin American Books. An Annotated Bibliography*. Center for Inter-American Relations: New York, 1974.

Jason Wilson, 'Spanish American Literature in Translation', *SLAS Bulletin*, 22, January 1975, pp.14–18.

Bradley A. Shaw, *Latin American Literature in English Translation. An Annotated Bibliography*. New York University Press: New York, 1976. 624 items listed.

Juan R. and Patricia Freudenthal (eds.), *Index to Anthologies of Latin American Literature in English Translation*. G. K. Hall: Boston, 1977.

Bradly A. Shaw, *Latin American Literature in English, 1975–1978*. Supplement to *Review* 24, 1979.

Graciela Corvalán, *Latin American Women in English Translation: a Bibliography*. Latin American Studies Center: Los Angeles, 1980.

Pedro Shimose, *Diccionario de autores iberoamericanos*. Ministerio de Asuntos Exteriores: Madrid, 1982.

Solena Bryant, *Brazil*. Clio Press: Oxford, 1983.

Carmen Vásquez, 'Bibliographical Résumé of English Translations', in *Cultural Identity in Latin America*, UNESCO, 1986, pp.201–4.

Daniel Maratos and Marnesba Hill, *Escritores de la diáspora cubana. Manual bibliográfica*. The Scarecrow Press: Metuchen, NJ, 1986.

Bibliography in John King (ed.), *Modern Latin American Fiction: a Survey*. Faber & Faber: London, 1987.

Irwing Stern (ed.), *Dictionary of Brazilian Literature*. Greenwood Press: New York, 1988.

Diane E. Marking (ed.), *Women Writers of Spanish America. An Annotated Bio-Bibliographical Guide*. Greenwood Press: New York, 1987.